The PhD

Palgrave Research Skills

Authoring a PhD
The Foundations of Research (2nd edn)
Getting to Grips with Doctoral Research
Getting Published
The Good Supervisor (2nd edn)
Maximizing the Impacts of University Research
The PhD Viva
The Postgraduate Research Handbook (2nd edn)
Structuring Your Research Thesis
The Professional Doctorate

Palgrave Teaching and Learning

Series Editor: **Sally Brown**

Facilitating Workshops
For the Love of Learning
Leading Dynamic Seminars
Learning, Teaching and Assessment in Higher Education
Live Onlne Learning

Further titles are in preparation

For a complete listing of all our titles in this area please visit
www.palgrave.com/studyskills

The PhD Viva

How to Prepare For Your Oral Examination

Peter Smith

First published 2014 by
PALGRAVE MACMILLAN

Palgrave Macmillan in the UK is an imprint of Macmillan Publishers Limited, registered in England, company number 785998, of Houndmills, Basingstoke, Hampshire RG21 6XS.

Palgrave Macmillan in the US is a division of St Martin's Press LLC, 175 Fifth Avenue, New York, NY 10010.

Palgrave Macmillan is the global academic imprint of the above companies and has companies and representatives throughout the world.

Palgrave® and Macmillan® are registered trademarks in the United States, the United Kingdom, Europe and other countries

ISBN: 978-1-137-39576-4

This book is printed on paper suitable for recycling and made from fully managed and sustained forest sources. Logging, pulping and manufacturing processes are expected to conform to the environmental regulations of the country of origin.

A catalogue record for this book is available from the British Library.

A catalog record for this book is available from the Library of Congress.

Printed in China

To my lovely wife Marie

Contents

List of Figures and Tables

Figures

Tables

Acknowledgements

I would like to thank the many students who have been kind enough to share their doctoral journeys with me. I am privileged to have experienced their highs and lows, and their ultimate triumph as they graduate. This book would not have been possible without them.

In particular, I would wish to thank the following PhD and DProf graduates who allowed me to use their work and their experiences in this book: Beatriz Africano, William Ault, Matthew Bartley, Jeremy Brown, Ronan Fitzpatrick, Joan Goss, Marianne Hill, Patrick Routledge, Patricia Stenhouse, Jane Thompson and Cate Watkinson. I would also like to thank my many colleagues who have contributed in numerous ways to the material and experiences on which this book is based. Many thanks also to Marian van Bakel, Jenna Condie, Thomas Geernaert and Simon Leather for allowing me to use their material. I would also like to thank the reviewers of the draft manuscript; they raised some very useful points and were generous in their comments.

1 Introduction

On completion of this chapter you will:

▶ understand the structure of this book, and how you will be able to use it to prepare for your viva
▶ start to understand the nature of the doctorate and the viva
▶ start to become confident about your viva, and begin to make preparations for it
▶ be thinking positively about all the work that you have done, and starting to look forward to your viva

1.1 Chapter overview

"The day of my PhD viva was one of the most special days of my life. Yes I was nervous, but once I settled into it, I started to really enjoy the experience. When else do you get the chance to talk about your work (and nothing else) for a couple of hours with a few people who are really interested in what you have done?"

Welcome to this book.

So you're getting close to the end of your PhD, and the mystical and scary thing known as a viva is coming up on the horizon. You probably realise how important your viva is, and you want to make sure that you prepare properly for it. That's what this book is about. I'm going to try to help you as much as I can in your preparations for your viva by covering every possible aspect and angle.

The approach taken in the book is a mix of accounts of my own personal experience, supplemented by the comments and experiences of several of the students I have supervised and examined, and whose vivas I have chaired, over the past 30 years or so. I have also read anything and everything I could find about the PhD viva while writing this book to be sure that my writing is grounded in the literature. This reading is backed up by references which are cited throughout the text and listed at the end of the book. I also include, where relevant, some examples of university regulations and documentation relating to the PhD and its assessment. I hope what I have produced is a practical text which will be of real use to you during your preparations for your viva.

I have sat in on many (probably over 100) PhD examinations. Sometimes I have been the examiner, questioning the student on their PhD thesis. Sometimes I have been the supervisor, almost as nervous as my student, observing the proceedings and hoping that all goes well. And sometimes

I have chaired the examination, trying to ensure that the student is treated fairly, that the examiners are able to ask all their questions, and that university regulations are followed. Along the way I have seen many students pass, have had to ask some to make changes to their thesis, and have also seen some examinations which have not gone so well. I have seen students elated, perform well or not so well, and some have burst into tears. I have dealt with some very fair and experienced examiners, and some who were not so reasonable. I have seen examiners disagree, and had to try to resolve this, and I have dealt with appeals against the decision of examiners.

I have attended PhD examinations in computing, mathematics, engineering, business, sociology, history, pharmacy and education, to name a few. I have presided over examinations of professional doctorate students and practice-based PhDs in art, where the students show us the artwork they have produced. I have dealt with the examinations of students of all ages, from candidates in their 20s through to their 80s. I have also chaired the university research degrees committee and was thus privy to the deliberations relating to hundreds of PhD examinations across a range of disciplines. I have examined at over 30 universities in the UK, Ireland, Hong Kong and Spain. As a consequence, I thought it was about time that I used my experience to write a text on the mythical viva.

I hope that this book will provide you with a valuable resource as you approach your viva, or oral examination as it is also known. The book is aimed primarily at students, but I hope that it will also be of use to those of you who are supervisors of PhD students. Throughout the text I will draw on real case studies and student experiences of the PhD viva, so that you can see how others approached their oral examination and learn from their experiences.

I recognise that the format of the oral examination, as well as the thesis, varies from country to country and from one discipline to another. I have tried to write this book so that it is not specific to one country or discipline. Where necessary, I have pointed out any differences in format or style.

One aim of the book is to make your viva a positive experience. You should look forward to your oral examination, and enjoy it on the day. It is one of the few times in your life when you will have the opportunity to talk about your work with a small group of interested people. You have worked hard for your PhD, and should be proud of what you have achieved. The viva gives you the opportunity to really show what you have done, and how useful and important it is.

I have approached this book in a positive manner, to try to help you do the same for your own viva. My aim is to ensure that you present yourself and your work in the best possible way in your preparations for, and during, your viva; and that this results in an enjoyable and positive experience for you and your examiners.

I have written the book in an easy-to-read, personal style, rather than as a piece of academic work. It could be read at any point in your doctoral studies. Indeed, the earlier you start your preparations, the better. I have sprinkled quotes from students (and some from fellow supervisors and examiners) throughout the book; these are included in italics in every chapter.

1.2 The nature of the doctorate

A doctorate is the highest level of academic qualification, and is normally awarded for the equivalent of three years of full-time study. The term 'doctorate' refers to the level of the qualification. There are many different forms of doctorate; the most traditional being the PhD or Doctor of Philosophy. However, in recent years, a number of different forms of doctorate have emerged, including the DBA (Doctor of Business Administration), EdD (Doctor of Education) and EngD (Engineering Doctorate). Many of these new doctorates are professional doctorates (Smith et al., 2011; Thompson et al., 2012; Fulton et al., 2013) which enable experienced professionals to study for a higher degree. Professional doctorates usually include a taught element at the start of the programme, followed by a work-based research project. Within this book we will use the term PhD, but much of what you read is applicable to any form of doctorate. Where there are differences which arise for different forms of doctorate, such as the professional doctorate, these will be made clear to you.

No matter which form of doctorate you are undertaking, or where you are studying it, the standard is the same. All doctorates culminate in a major research project which is expected to make a 'contribution to knowledge'. The contribution to knowledge is the fundamental difference between the PhD and other postgraduate qualifications at Master's level. Making a contribution to knowledge implies that, within your project, you are doing something which hasn't been done before, adding to your subject in some modest way, and undertaking a research project which is new and produces unique results. Assessing the contribution to knowledge is one of the prime functions of the viva, or oral examination. You shouldn't panic when thinking about how you will make a contribution to knowledge. It isn't as daunting as it sounds. In the chapters which follow I will explore the concept of 'contribution to knowledge' and how you can demonstrate it to your examiners.

As well as the expectation of a contribution to knowledge within your PhD, you will also be expected to demonstrate the following knowledge and skills within your thesis and your viva:

- *Criticality*. As a PhD candidate you are expected to be able to think critically, and to demonstrate this within your writing.
- *Write academically*. There is a particular style to academic writing, which you will have developed during your research and in the process

of writing your thesis. Your writing needs to be concise, rigorous and supported by references to the academic literature of your subject. It also needs to conform to the writing style of your discipline, drawing from, and engaging with, the 'academic discourse' and terminology which others working in your subject area will recognise. Every statement that you make in your thesis needs to be justified, either by one or more references to the work of others, or by your own findings and data.

- *Subject knowledge.* You will be expected to show in your thesis, and during the discussions in your viva, that you understand the main and most recent works within your subject, and the broader area that surrounds it. This may seem daunting. However, you will have been reading relevant research papers throughout your studies, so you will have built this knowledge up over the period of your PhD.
- *Research methods.* You need to show that you understand the research approaches which are used within your subject and that you have used relevant and sensible approaches within your PhD research. You will need to justify your choice of method(s) in your thesis, and in the viva, and that you have used your chosen approach consistently and correctly.
- *Ethics.* You will need to show that you have followed sound ethical principles and acquired necessary approvals for your study, and that you have considered the ethical, social, and environmental implications of your work.
- *Communication skills.* Your thesis will demonstrate your writing and presentation skills. Your viva will test your ability to present, discuss and defend your work to a small group of peers.

I will discuss each of these elements of the PhD in more detail in the chapters that follow. This means that I will continually return to these topics, and I expect you to do the same. Each time, you will be further strengthening the groundwork for your examination so that by the time you enter that examination room you will feel confident that you are fully prepared for the examiners and their questions.

"I was a little disappointed when my viva came to an end as I was really enjoying the experience."

1.3 The viva

The PhD viva remains shrouded in secrecy, with its own mythology. Debate still goes on as to the exact purpose and form of the viva, and practice can, and does, vary. In recent years much has been done to standardise the viva, and to ensure consistency of treatment.

In the viva, a small examination team questions the candidate on the work presented in the thesis. In some countries (particularly in mainland Europe), the oral examination is a public event, whereas in others, including the UK, it is much more closed. In recent years, standards have been developed to ensure consistency of approach in the oral examination. Much has been written about the nature of the PhD viva. Research in this area covers doctoral standards (Morley et al., 2002; Carter and Whittaker, 2009), the nature and variability of the oral examination (Tinkler and Jackson, 2000), selection of doctoral examiners (Joyner, 2003), and the analysis of personal experiences of doctoral candidates (Wallace, 2003).

The viva has several purposes:

- To ensure that the work is your own.
- To ensure that you understand the work that you have done, and the broader literature from your subject.
- To discuss the contribution to knowledge made by your work.
- To enable the examiners to question you on any area of your work that they may have concerns about.
- To evaluate your ability to discuss and communicate your work, and defend your arguments and conclusions.
- As a development experience in itself.
- As a 'rite of passage' or acceptance (by the examiners) of you (the candidate) as an academic peer.
- In the case of a borderline thesis, the viva has a very important role in deciding the overall outcome of the assessment.

The viva panel will be a small group of individuals who are knowledgeable in your field of study, and are experienced in examining. The viva then takes the form of a discussion with the panel, who will ask you questions about your work. After the discussion the panel will decide whether the degree of PhD should be awarded to you, whether you should rewrite sections of your thesis, or whether you need to undertake further research work. The panel makes a recommendation to the university where you are registered, and it is the university research degrees committee, or academic board, which will take the final decision and make the award of the degree.

1.4 Structure of the book

In Chapter 2, I discuss the role and nature of the PhD viva in some detail. I define the purpose of the PhD viva and what it is setting out to assess.

I make the distinction between assessment of the thesis and assessment of you, the candidate. In order to do so, the concepts of the doctorate and doctoral standards are explored. This leads to a detailed discussion of the concepts of 'contribution to knowledge', 'criticality' and 'independent thinking'. The oral examination process is explained, and alternative models for the viva are discussed with reference to the approaches taken in different countries. A typical timetable for a PhD viva is set out, giving some regulatory frameworks for the viva as examples. The findings and conclusions of recent research into the PhD viva by a range of academic authors are reviewed.

Chapter 3 explains the constitution of the PhD viva panel, including the roles of the examiners (internal and external), the independent chair, you – the candidate – and the supervisor. The expectations of each player are examined in some detail, and the importance of choice of examiners is discussed. Tips on how to explore the previous research experience of the examiners are given. This chapter also includes discussion as to whether your supervisor should be present in your viva, how that decision is made, and their role if they do attend. This chapter also briefly refers to the composition of the panel in different countries.

Chapter 4 provides vital tips on how, and when, to start preparing for your viva. This includes tips on writing the thesis with your examiners and the viva in mind, preparing for your viva in the months before, and how to prepare as the event draws closer, in the weeks and days before your viva. I give advice on reviewing the work that you have done, how and when to re-read your thesis, defining and explaining the contribution made, the literature reviewed and the methodological approach taken. Differences between disciplines are covered, including the possibility of preparing a formal presentation, which is becoming the norm in some subjects. The custom of having a practice or 'mock' viva is discussed, as is the importance of presenting work throughout the PhD process in seminars, conferences and so on. The chapter makes use of real case-study material drawn from students on how they prepared for their own PhD viva. Practical tips, such as preparing chapter summaries and the answers to questions, are given. The issue of your own well-being and how to prepare emotionally and physically for your viva is also covered.

Chapter 5 covers typical viva questions and how best to answer them. It is, of course, not possible to predict detailed questions relating to the specifics of your work. However, this chapter addresses some of the likely questions that you may face during your viva, and how best you might go about answering them. I also cover the nature of the questioning process, how to handle tricky and difficult questions, and how to interact with the examiners. The concept of 'defending' your work is discussed. Tips are given on what to do if you don't understand a question.

In Chapter 6 I play out an entire viva, using examples drawn from real student examinations. I explain the preliminary stages of the viva, including the examiners' private pre-meeting and the role of preliminary reports. I then go on to present some possible situations that might arise during your own viva so that you can be better prepared for these. Finally, I cover the post-viva private meeting of the examiners in which they deliberate on the outcome of the PhD examination.

A viva can result in several possible outcomes, ranging from a straight Pass through various levels of amendment and revisions to Re-submission, the award of MPhil or (very rarely) outright Fail. Each of the possible outcomes that you could face is discussed in some detail in Chapter 7, with reference to typical university regulations. The questions which are often asked of examiners on the assessment documentation are used as an illustration so that you can think about how you might prepare with these questions in mind. I also give advice on how to take the next steps after the outcome has been decided, including your approach to amendments, further work or a further examination. Appeal processes and the grounds on which a candidate might appeal are discussed. Finally, recovering from the viva and dealing with the sense of achievement and/or anti-climax are covered.

Chapter 8 presents ten case studies of students and their viva experiences. These are drawn from real students with whom I have had personal involvement. The case studies first present a brief background to the candidate in order to set the context. The candidate then discusses, in their own words, how they prepared for the viva, how the viva experience was for them, the nature of the questions asked and the questioning process, and the outcome. Where there was a need for revisions to the thesis, these are also discussed. The case studies are analysed and a series of lessons drawn out. The case studies cover a range of disciplines and a range of outcomes. I hope that, through these case studies, you will gain a deeper understanding of the entire viva process so that you can locate your own doctoral study within the examples and use them to help you prepare for your own viva.

The final chapter, Chapter 9, draws together all of the main points raised throughout the text and summarises them as a checklist, which I hope you will find useful in your viva preparations. I conclude with some final reflections of my own experiences of PhD examinations.

The book is supported by a full set of current references, and some websites which I think you will find useful.

1.5 Exercises

I would like you to start this book in a positive frame of mind. You have done a lot of work for your PhD and you should be proud of your achievements. Start off with these simple exercises.

▶ Think of all of the positive aspects of your PhD study (see Figure 1.1). What have you achieved? Think of all the hard work you have done.

Figure 1.1   Think of the positive aspects of your PhD

▶ Write down the three accomplishments of which you are most proud. Why are you proud of these?

▶ Write down a list of the types of people who will be interested in reading your thesis. Which group of people will be interested in reading about what you have done? Think of academics and other researchers who are working in a similar field to you. Think about practitioners or others who might have a use for your work. Think about how useful your work will be to them.

▶ Focus on the end. Think about collecting your final hard-bound thesis (complete with its beautiful gold lettering) for presentation to your university library. Think also about graduation and how you will feel when you formally receive your PhD, are handed your certificate and can call yourself 'Doctor'.

These exercises should start you off in a positive frame of mind for the rest of the book and the exercises and preparations which follow.

Summary

This chapter has introduced the book and given you an idea of how I will set out to try and help you in your preparations for your viva. I have given you a quick overview of the nature of the doctorate and the viva.

Your viva is a very important part of your PhD. It is an examination and, like any other examination, you need to spend time preparing for it. If you prepare properly and thoroughly you will enter the examination in the knowledge and confidence that you are ready to perform well. After all, it is your PhD and you have spent several years studying for it. You will know exactly what you have done, how (and why) you have done it and what it has produced in terms of that 'magic' contribution to knowledge. You will then be in a position to enjoy your viva.

The day of your viva is an important one. It should be a day that you look forward to, not fear. You should enter that examination room confident and proud of what you have achieved. You will then be able to have a good discussion with your examiners, and to enjoy that discussion. The aim of this book is to prepare you for that important day and to ensure that you have considered every aspect of your PhD study when preparing for your viva. I hope you enjoy reading the book and that you find it useful. As well as my own thoughts and experiences, the book also contains lessons and experiences from real PhD candidates who I have supervised and examined in the past. I hope that the use of real case studies will be useful for you.

Be honest, thoughtful and passionate about your research area. Interest, passion and authenticity will keep you motivated through difficult times, and will make your arguments more convincing, both in the way you write them, and how you ultimately speak them during your oral examination.

> *"Good preparation means you need not fear the viva. It can, and will, be an enjoyable experience for you!"*

Good luck and I hope that you enjoy the book and find it of use in your viva preparations.

Peter Smith

Professor Peter Smith
peter.smith@sunderland.ac.uk

If you have any comments or questions and want to email about any aspect of your PhD study, please do so. I will do my best to reply.

2 The PhD viva

On completion of this chapter you will:

▶ understand the standard that you are required to reach for the award of your PhD
▶ start to be able to define and defend your contribution to knowledge
▶ understand what is meant by criticality and be able to demonstrate critical and independent thinking
▶ understand the role and structure of the PhD viva, including the alternative approaches taken in different countries
▶ recognise a typical timetable for a PhD viva
▶ understand current research into the PhD assessment process

2.1 Chapter overview

This chapter discusses the role and nature of the PhD viva in some detail. I start by defining the purpose of the PhD viva and what it is setting out to assess. I make the distinction between the assessment of the thesis and the assessment of you, the candidate. In order to do so, I first explore the concept of the doctorate and doctoral standards. This leads to a discussion of the concepts of 'contribution to knowledge', 'criticality' and 'independent thinking'. The oral examination process is explained, leading to a discussion of alternative models for the viva with reference to the approaches taken in different countries, including the private and public defence systems. A typical timetable for a PhD viva is set out, and a sample regulatory framework is used as an example. The findings and conclusions of recent research into the PhD viva by a range of academic authors are reviewed, giving you pointers for further reading into the topic, should you wish to do so.

2.2 Doctoral standards

Let's start by considering what is meant by doctoral standards. There are several definitions. For example the Quality Assurance Agency for Higher Education (QAA) sets standards for university level education in the UK, and has established a 'Framework for Higher Education Qualification in England Wales and Northern Ireland' (QAA, 2008). The QAA document sets out the outcomes that should be achieved for the award of degrees at Bachelor, Master's and Doctoral level. Similar agencies exist in other countries of the world. Although there are some small differences between these definitions of doctoral standards, there is general agreement that a doctorate should include achievement in the areas outlined in Table 2.1. (Note that the interpretation in Table 2.1 is my own.)

Area	Standard
Contribution to knowledge	The fundamental requirement of the doctorate is that it will lead to the creation and interpretation of new knowledge which is of sufficient quality to satisfy peer review within the relevant discipline, extend the forefront of that discipline, and be worthy of publication.
Grasp of the subject	The candidate should be able to demonstrate a deep understanding of the body of knowledge relating to their topic of study. This should have been approached in a systematic manner and demonstrate up-to-date knowledge of the state of the art and recent developments in the field of study.
Independence as a researcher	The candidate should be able to demonstrate that they can operate as an independent researcher. That is, they must be able to show that they have the skills and abilities to conceptualise, design and implement a substantial research project which has resulted in the generation of new knowledge at the forefront of their chosen discipline. They must also demonstrate that they are able to take their own decisions during the course of that project, adjusting the project design in the light of unforeseen problems, and making use of the best available data.
Research methodology	A PhD is a research degree, and candidates will need to be able to demonstrate that they have chosen, and used, research methods which are acceptable within their own discipline. This will require a detailed understanding of applicable techniques for research and the ability to apply these in a systematic and rigorous manner. This includes consideration of the ethical and wider implications of the research study and the limitations of the work.
Critical thinking	The candidate needs to be able to show that they can think critically, that they carefully question and analyse their own work and the conclusions of others, and are able to analyse and present arguments in a clear and logical manner.
Communication skills	A doctoral candidate must be able to demonstrate that they are able to communicate their findings verbally and through their written work, in the form of a thesis, to their academic peers and to a more general audience.
Substantial project	A PhD is awarded for a substantial piece of work over a prolonged period of study. This is normally 3 or more years of full-time work, and results in the production of a substantial thesis in the order of 40,000 to 80,000 words, and longer in some instances. (*Note*: this is dependent upon the academic discipline of the thesis.)

Table 2.1   A summary of doctoral standards

Let's now discuss each of the concepts in Table 2.1 in some detail, and consider how you might approach thinking about them as you prepare for your viva.

Contribution to knowledge. This is probably the most important concept because it is the contribution to knowledge which, more than anything else, distinguishes the PhD from a Master's degree. It is also the concept that worries most candidates, who find it difficult to understand. Taken literally, 'contribution to knowledge' means that the research has resulted in something new, some findings which weren't known before this study, and some new knowledge which extends the subject discipline. And that is all true. A PhD study should do all of those things.

. However, it also needs to be said that a PhD is not the same as a Nobel Prize (Mullins and Kiley, 2002). If it was, there wouldn't be many people with PhDs. There are thousands of PhDs awarded around the world every year, and each of those PhD graduates has made a small, yet significant, contribution to knowledge within their own field of study. Basically, you need to show that your study builds on the existing literature in the field, that it results in some new findings that someone else from your subject (and that includes, especially, your examiners) will find interesting and useful, and that, most importantly, they will learn something new from reading your thesis. This can also be called 'originality' or 'novelty'. It is very important that you are able to clearly articulate your contribution in a concise and focused way. This is something that we will return to several times, starting at the end of this chapter, by asking you to write down your contribution.

Grasp of the subject. It is important that you understand the literature which relates directly to your subject. During your viva you may also be asked to discuss background work, which may not relate directly to yours, but is nonetheless important in your subject. You will have a set of references within your thesis. These should include the seminal studies which underpin your work, and also the most recent and up-to-date pieces of research. You will need to read and re-read these as you approach your viva to ensure that you understand the main points of those pieces of work which are most important for your thesis. You will have your thesis with you during the viva, and will be able to refer to it, but it is important to be able to discuss some of the most relevant papers which you have read and reviewed during the course of your PhD.

Independence as a researcher. During your viva you will need to be able to demonstrate that it is you, and not your supervisor, who has driven and done the work. It is likely that you will be asked to explain why you took certain decisions during the course of your PhD project, and what the implications of those decisions were. Some of the decisions that you took may, in hindsight, have not been the best. It is acceptable, and indeed good, to admit to this, and to show that you have learned from your PhD experience. One purpose of the PhD is to train candidates as independent researchers, so that they can go on to undertake, lead and supervise research projects in the future. It is useful to keep a project diary, or use a notebook, to record the decisions that you take during your PhD studies so that you can remind yourself later of the reasons why you made a particular choice or took a particular decision.

Research methodology. More than anything, a PhD is a training in research. You will need to be able to demonstrate, and justify, the overall methodological framework which you have chosen to follow, and the methods which you have used within your study. You need to understand the difference between methodology and methods. Many students use these terms interchangeably, and they mean different things. The methodology is the overall approach taken by the candidate, such as action research or grounded theory. The method is a specific approach taken, such as a questionnaire or focus groups. In the arts the methodology may be considered to be the artist's own practice. It is important that you understand the distinction between the methodology and methods within the context of the discourse in your own academic discipline. If this is something that you are unsure about you should discuss it with your supervisor in the period leading up to your viva.

Critical thinking. You need to be able to show that you have developed the skill of critical thinking. This should be coming through in the way that you have written your thesis. Being critical means not simply accepting the conclusions of other writers without evaluating their arguments and the evidence that they provide to underpin those arguments. Critical writing should display balanced reasoning, discussing why the conclusions of others may be accepted in the context of your study or why they may need to be treated with some caution. This implies a clear presentation of your own arguments, leading to a well-argued and balanced conclusion; including recognising the limitations of your own work. It is critical writing which raises a thesis to doctoral level. Descriptive writing simply summarises and describes the work of others without going beyond giving a straightforward account of the work. Critical writing requires thinking, analysis, synthesis and reasoning. You need to be able to get past simple description and show that you are capable of deep understanding and analysis of your own findings and those of other researchers in your field.

Communication skills. This covers all aspects of communication, written and oral. Your written communication skills are assessed when the examiners read your thesis. One of the roles of the viva is to assess your verbal communication skills. You need to be able to discuss your work with your peers in a clear and confident manner. QAA (2008) refers to the candidate being able to: *'make informed judgements on complex issues in specialist fields, often in the absence of complete data, and be able to communicate their ideas and conclusions clearly and effectively to specialist and non-specialist audiences.'* For research to make any real impact, it needs to be communicated as widely as possible. It thus follows that communication is a vital research skill which warrants exploration and assessment during the oral examination. In later chapters of the book I will discuss ways in which you can practise your communication skills. At the time of writing (2014) there is a move towards ensuring that research has impact on business, industry, health, well-being and society in general, as characterised in the UK by the Research Excellence Framework (REF) (www.ref.ac.uk).

Substantial project. This should be self-evident. You have produced a substantial thesis, which is likely to be in the order of 40,000 to 80,000 words, reporting on a large body of research work. You must check the actual word limits in the regulations of your own university. You will have spent upwards of three years' full-time, or perhaps more years as a part-time student, working on your thesis. Your viva is the culmination of all the time you have spent studying, and a rare and precious opportunity to discuss your work with a small group of peers and to demonstrate everything that you have done. It is easy to start to worry about the viva, and it is understandable that you might do so. But you need to think positively about all of the work that you have done. It will certainly be substantial, and you should be proud of that, and prepare for your viva in a confident and positive manner.

2.3 The viva

I start this section by defining the purpose of the PhD viva and what it is setting out to assess. A distinction is made between the assessment of your thesis and the assessment of you, the candidate. The oral examination process is also explained.

> In the final part of the assessment, the candidate defends his or her research in the viva, and demonstrates deep knowledge and understanding of the field of study, and originality of thought, either in the creation of new knowledge or in the novel application of existing knowledge. (QAA, 2011)

As stated in Chapter 1 (and repeated here, as I feel it is important to reiterate the point), the viva has several purposes:

- To ensure that the work is your own.
- To ensure that you understand the work that you have done, and the broader literature from your subject.

- To discuss the contribution to knowledge made by your work.
- To enable the examiners to question you on any area of your work that they may have concerns about.
- To evaluate your ability to discuss and communicate your work, and defend your arguments and conclusions.
- As a development experience in itself.
- As a 'rite of passage' or acceptance (by the examiners) of you (the candidate) as an academic peer.
- In the case of a borderline thesis, the viva has a very important role in deciding the overall outcome of the assessment.

Tinkler and Jackson (2008) surveyed a number of examiners and concluded that there was no consensus concerning the purposes of a PhD viva. They categorised the purposes that were mentioned by examiners into three main functions: (i) assessment, (ii) development of the candidate and their work, and (iii) ritual (that is, a gatekeeping process which allows entry into 'the academy').

Your viva panel will be a small group of individuals who are knowledgeable in your field of study, and are experienced in examining. The viva then takes the form of a discussion with the panel, who will ask you questions about your work. After the discussion the panel will decide whether the degree of PhD should be awarded to you, whether you should re-write sections of your thesis, or whether you need to undertake further research work. The panel make a recommendation to the university where you are registered, and it is the university's research degrees committee, or academic board, who will take the final decision and make the award of the degree.

All universities are required to have clear procedures for the oral examination to ensure that it is carried out rigorously, fairly and consistently. There is general agreement that this must always include input from an external examiner. There will be a period of time between the submission of your thesis and the viva taking place. This should normally be no longer than two or three months, and many universities have a regulation which states that vivas must be 'carried out to a reasonable timescale', as suggested by QAA (2012).

Assessment procedures are defined in the UK system (QAA, 2012) as follows:

- The examination is always in two parts; the first is the examination of the thesis, during which the examiners read the thesis and form an independent view of the candidate's work, and the second is the oral examination (which is also commonly known as a *viva voce* or a viva).
- There must always be at least two 'appropriately qualified' (in terms of experience, academic qualifications and subject expertise) examiners.

- There must always be at least one external examiner within the examination team. An external examiner is external to the university where the candidate is registered. The insistence on an external examiner is to ensure independence in consideration of the candidate for the award of the degree.
- None of the candidate's supervisors can be appointed as an examiner. This is a relatively new standard. Until the 1990s, it was the norm for the supervisor to be the internal examiner. This is now seen as a conflict of interests, and no longer allowed in the UK.
- It is not acceptable to appoint an internal or external examiner who has had a close working relationship with the candidate, such as co-authoring or collaborative involvement in the candidate's work, or has previously acted as a supervisor for the work. It is also not seen as appropriate to appoint an examiner whose own work is the focus of the research project. Again, this is to ensure independence and to guard against any potential conflict of interests.
- Examiners submit separate, independent written reports before the viva and a joint report after it. It is important the examiners submit separate reports prior to the viva, as this records their initial and independent views on the thesis, and guards against the possibility of the views of one examiner prejudicing the views of another examiner.

In other words, the viva is a full and formal part of the assessment of your doctorate. It is separate from the assessment of the thesis, and yet it is used, at least in part, to assess the thesis. It is possible (though unlikely) for a candidate to produce an excellent thesis, and yet perform poorly in the viva if they are not able to adequately present, explain and discuss their work with the examiners. It is also possible (and this happens quite often) for a candidate who has produced a thesis with some flaws, and hence borderline in terms of passing, to discuss their work very well during the viva, and thus retrieve the situation to pass overall. (In such a case I would expect the candidate to be required to make some revisions to the thesis.) Tinkler and Jackson (2008) highlight the role of the viva in determining an outcome in borderline cases.

2.4 Different models for the viva

A number of alternative models for the viva exist, and the format of the viva and the examination process vary from country to country. In the UK, the doctoral viva is usually a 'closed' examination, at which only the candidate, the examiners, and an independent Chair are present (QAA, 2011). In many universities the candidate's supervisor may, with the permission of the candidate, be present to observe the examination.

This general model of a closed examination has been compared (Tinkler and Jackson, 2004) with some non-UK European viva models. These models often include a 'public defence', where the candidate may invite family and friends to join the audience. The event is as much a celebration of the candidate's work and the fact that they have reached the end of that journey, as it is a defence of the thesis.

On two occasions I attended a public defence at a university in Spain. I will describe one of those experiences here. The candidate was registered for a European doctorate, which meant that he had to present his thesis in at least two European languages. The thesis had been written in Spanish, and I was sent an English translation. The examination panel consisted of four external examiners. Two were from Spain, I was from England and one examiner came from Portugal. The oral examination took place in a lecture theatre, which was full. The candidate's family, friends and other students all attended. The candidate made a formal presentation, showing slides on two screens. On one screen the slides were in Spanish, while on the other screen they were displayed in English (largely for my benefit). The presentation was in Spanish.

At the end of the presentation each of the examiners asked the candidate questions in their own language, and the candidate answered in that language. We had been told beforehand that we were expected to ask a small number of questions; perhaps three or four. The audience were then invited to ask questions, and a small number of people did so. Everyone was then asked to leave, and the examiners discussed the outcome of the examination. In this case we were asked to grade the outcome; the two grades being Pass or Pass with Honours. We were all very impressed by the work and felt that the candidate's contribution was substantial. We noted that he had published a significant number of papers prior to submission of the thesis. Having examined the criteria for the award, we unanimously agreed to award PhD with Honours.

I have also taken part, as external examiner, in a number of PhD vivas in computer science and engineering in Hong Kong. In those examinations there were two external examiners (one from Hong Kong and one from another country; in these cases, me), an internal examiner and a Chair. The candidate was required to make a 30-minute Microsoft® Powerpoint presentation at the start of the viva. The presentation was a public event, with other students from the department invited and allowed to ask questions. After the candidate had finished their presentation, and everyone had asked their questions, the audience were asked to leave and the formal viva took place. This took a similar format to the vivas I am used to within the UK system, although the questioning would often not take as long because many of the possible questions had been covered by the candidate during their presentation.

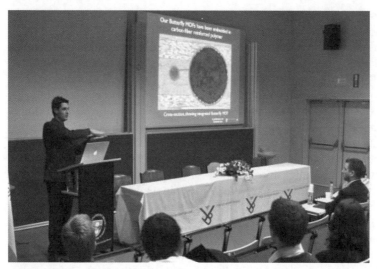

Figure 2.1   A thesis defence

Many thanks to Dr Thomas Geernaert for permission to include this photograph.

Figure 2.1 shows a PhD defence in Vrije Universiteit Brussels. This is Thomas Geernaert successfully defending his PhD thesis for the award of the degree of Doctor in Engineering. His PhD research focused on 'Micro-structured fibre Bragg grating sensors: from fibre design to sensor implementation' and 'the goal of this work was to design, simulate, fabricate, characterize and implement a temperature-insensitive optical fibre sensor for hydrostatic pressure and transverse strain.'

A fascinating account – 'Defending your PhD thesis: the Dutch way' – by Dr Marian van Bakel describes her PhD defence in the Netherlands. It is reproduced opposite with her kind permission. (See Figure 2.2 for a picture of the examination panel.)

In most cases the candidate does not know whether they have passed until after the final assessment in the viva. The viva is an integral part of the whole assessment, so it would not be appropriate to signal to the candidate that they have passed until the viva has ended. However, I have been present in a few vivas (albeit many years ago) where the external examiner has indicated to the candidate at the start of the viva that they feel the thesis is of the right standard and that they expect the result to be positive. This would not be deemed best practice today.

In some countries, Australia in particular, there is currently no requirement for a viva. The examiners read the thesis, and send written reports to the university, giving a recommendation concerning the award or otherwise of the degree. A viva is usually only called for if the examiners have concerns with the work.

Defending your PhD thesis: the Dutch way

"Today a year ago I was defending my PhD thesis at Radboud University Nijmegen. It was quite a happening, what with the pedel [beadle], seven examiners in full academic dress, two paranimfen to support me, and all my friends and family present. This, of course, is not how it happens around the globe. For example, in the UK it is known as a viva (officially viva voce – Latin for 'by live voice'), which is an oral examination with two or three examiners that usually takes place in private and can last very long – as long as they can think of questions to ask you. In the Netherlands the PhD has to be published as a book before the defence takes place – in Germany this happens after the defence. You have a year to do that and only then you are officially awarded your degree."

"The Dutch PhD defence is very formal: there is a protocol to be followed, stipulating what happens at every step, what you should say at the beginning and at the end, and how you should address your opponents. For example, professors are addressed as hooggeleerde opponens whereas those who 'only' have a PhD are addressed as hooggeachte opponens. By the way, this is why it is a very good idea to prepare pieces of paper with the name of each opponent and the way you should address them. Believe me, when you are standing there you won't remember which form of address to use for which opponent."

"One of the quirks of the Dutch PhD defence is that you have two paranimfen at your side to answer questions for you if you get unwell, or even to physically defend you if the argument gets out of hand. Happily both things don't really happen any more – although paranimfen are still allowed to speak on your behalf, the accuracy of their left hook is never tested. Nowadays paranimfen are better compared to best men or bridesmaids; they support you in the period leading to the defence and arrange all kinds of practicalities during the day itself. No need any more to choose tall, burly paranimfen!"

"Another interesting aspect is the pedel or bedel [beadle] in English, who is the master of ceremonies at PhD examinations in the Netherlands (among other duties). She (in my case) carries the ceremonial mace and leads the external examiners to their place. She also is the one who comes back after an hour to rescue you, stamping the mace on the ground and calling Hora est before leading the examiners out again. And that is after exactly an hour – no matter who is speaking. In my case the last examiner had just begun asking his question, so he was rather abruptly cut off because the defence is then over (you are only allowed to finish your sentence). Because this bluntness is normal for PhD defences in the Netherlands and rather fits our image of being very direct, it was funny that many of my friends and family were quite shocked by it!"

"Hora est is when the fun begins – first with a laudatio (a speech by your supervisor), then a reception, and usually a party. Oh, and life without having to work on a PhD thesis!"

Figure 2.2   The examination panel in a public defence

Many thanks to Dr Marian van Bakel, for permission to include this photograph from her public defence.

2.5 A typical viva timetable

A typical timetable for a viva is set out in Figure 2.3. Let's examine each aspect of the schedule in some detail.

Private meeting of the examination panel (approximately one hour; prior to the viva)

The examiners will come together with the Chair to discuss their views on the thesis. Each examiner will give their thoughts on the work and which aspects they feel they should explore and question during the examination. They will then all discuss and agree a rough schedule for the viva, including what areas are to be explored with the candidate, and who will ask what questions. The Chair will also make some final checks on the room and arrange the seating to try to make the candidate feel as comfortable as possible. When they are ready they will invite the candidate to join them for the viva. It is difficult to predict how long this meeting may take, as it depends upon the views that the examiners have about the thesis. It would normally be between 30 minutes and one hour.

PhD Oral Examination Schedule

Candidate:	Hamid
Day:	Wednesday 18th December 2013
Location:	Sciences Complex, Henry Building, Room 101
	City Campus, Town A
Supervisor:	Professor A
Panel:	Professor B (External Examiner)
	Dr C (Internal Examiner)
	Professor D (Independent Chair)

Schedule

Wednesday 18th December 2013

10.00am	Private meeting of the examiners and independent Chair to discuss preliminary views on the candidate's thesis, and agree questions and format of the viva.
10.45am	Oral examination
12.45pm	Private meeting over buffet lunch to discuss the outcome.
1.30pm	Feedback to candidate

Figure 2.3   A typical viva schedule

The oral examination itself (approximately two hours)

I cover the detail of what might happen within your viva in other chapters of this book. Predicting the length of time that a viva will take is difficult, as it will vary from candidate to candidate, depending on the nature of the questions and the areas which the examiners wish to explore and discuss. The average time for a viva is likely to be around two hours, with some vivas taking three hours. Very few vivas will last less than two hours. It is unusual for a viva to last for longer than three hours, but it can, and does, happen.

"The viva was a complete unknown, so I was a little nervous. However this proved to be unfounded. My nerves dissipated quickly as the examiners made me feel at ease and were genuinely interested in the subject matter as we engaged in the discussion. I took on board their comments and challenged appropriately where I felt their view was not accurately portraying the essence of the argument. This was all exchanged in an amicable and professional manner throughout the viva leaving me feeling challenged but able to hold my ground and believing it was a shared process."

Private meeting of the examination panel (approximately 30 minutes to one hour; after the viva)

When the examiners have asked all of their questions and the viva is finished, the Chair will ask you to leave the examination room. The examiners will then discuss your performance in the viva, and come to a final recommendation. If there are revisions that they require you to make to the thesis, they will normally produce a list of these for you. This list may be produced during this private meeting, or the examiners may choose to produce it after the meeting and provide it to you in the days which follow. There will be a form that the examiners must complete to document their recommendation. All of these activities take time, while you are waiting nervously. This time can seem to last for ever. In practice it is likely to be 30 minutes to one hour. It can be very short if the examiners are in agreement and can quickly come to a decision.

Feedback

Once the examiners have come to a decision you will be asked to return to the examination room and they will inform you of their recommendation. Hopefully this is good news and you can go and celebrate!

Table 2.2 shows a timeline for the entire viva process.

Month	Event
0	Examiners approved by the university at least 6 months prior to thesis submission
6	Thesis submitted and sent to examiners
6.5	Date arranged for viva, shortly after examiners receive the thesis
7.5	Examiners read the thesis, complete their preliminary reports and send them to the university
8	Day of viva Examiners' private meeting Viva Private meeting; complete reports Relay informal outcome to candidate Return documentation to university
9	Research Degrees Committee consideration and decision
11–12	Make any revisions and submit final version of the thesis
12–13	Degree awarded, produce final hard-bound copy of thesis for the library
	Graduation!

Table 2.2   The timeline of a PhD viva

2.6 Learning outcomes

Some programmes express PhD study in terms of a series of learning out-comes. A sample set of learning outcomes is shown in Table 2.3. Learning outcomes are usually wider ranging than the specific requirements of the PhD, and cover the skills and abilities which the university expects each student to develop. They will often include elements which are additional to those which are assessed during the PhD viva, and are included here for illustration.

Background and purpose

These learning outcomes have been produced to help PhD students identify the skills and abilities that they can develop during their PhD studies. They will be of use to students, supervisors, tutors and those involved in the training of PhD students to help identify training and support needs. They provide a framework to support students so they can reflect on their progress and development over the course of their PhD studies. Not all outcomes are applicable to all PhD students, and each student should develop their own set of learning outcomes based on these, in discussion with their supervisory team.

Research

The student will be able to:

- identify an original topic for research to be explored and/or an original problem or issue to be addressed;
- underpin their research with a foundation of previous research and knowledge;
- design and implement a programme of research using appropriate methodologies;
- identify, search, access and assess appropriate research information within libraries or other relevant repositories;
- demonstrate practical, analytical and problem-solving skills;
- collect, record, manage, analyse and synthesise data;
- critically evaluate one's own work and the work of others;
- develop theoretical concepts, underpinned by sound academic theory and arguments;
- demonstrate originality and independent thinking, resulting in a unique contribution to knowledge.

Communication

The student will be able to:

- present, disseminate and defend their research using *appropriate* media including written reports, oral presentations, posters, and conference and academic journal contributions;
- communicate their work to specialist and more general audiences;
- present their completed research in the form of a thesis;
- discuss and defend their work during a *viva voce* examination;
- engage in the support of the learning of other students through teaching and demonstrating practice, where appropriate and when opportunities are available.

Table 2.3   Sample learning outcomes for a PhD programme (*continued overleaf*)

Research environment

The student will be able to:

- discuss relevant ethical and legal issues, and adhere to relevant ethical standards and codes of conduct;
- recognise any relevant health and safety issues, attend the required training programmes and apply the necessary procedures;
- demonstrate responsible and professional working practices during their research;
- demonstrate knowledge of the role of research funding and adhere to any contractual and funding requirements applicable to their own research study.

Personal qualities and transferrable skills

The student will be able to:

- plan and implement a detailed programme of research so as to complete their studies and submit their thesis within the specified and required period of enrolment;
- manage relationships, whether with their supervisors, other research team members, collaborators, funders and other research students;
- demonstrate independence, autonomy and flexibility;
- manage and develop their own learning by identifying areas for personal development and training needs;
- attend, and participate in, relevant training events;
- reflect and report on their progress, and discuss this in an honest way with their supervisors;
- use appropriate software packages to carry out relevant tasks;
- develop their own career aspirations.

Table 2.3 *continued*   Sample learning outcomes for a PhD programme

Professional doctorate programmes may require the student to satisfy the learning outcomes, in which case they may be assessed during the viva. You should check to see if this is the case in your own university, and whether it applies to your programme of study. I will include a set of professional doctorate learning outcomes and show how you might demonstrate that you have satisfied them in Chapter 4.

2.7   Research on the PhD examination process

Much has been written about the nature of the PhD viva. Research in this area covers doctoral standards (Morley et al., 2002; Carter and Whittaker, 2009), the nature and variability of the oral examination (Tinkler and Jackson, 2000), selection of doctoral examiners (Joyner, 2003), and the analysis of personal experiences of doctoral candidates (Wallace, 2003).

The *Journal of Graduation Education* published some early studies which explored the status of the UK PhD viva, stating that is can be a 'mysterious affair' (Burnham, 1994) and arguing that there was, at the time, a 'dearth of published material' on the subject (Baldacchino, 1994). In the past twenty years much work has been undertaken to de-mystify the process, to understand the dynamics involved and to ensure fairness and comparability of standards.

Tinkler and Jackson (2004, 2008) undertook very extensive research on the doctoral assessment process, surveying and interviewing candidates and academics across Britain over a four-year period. They concluded that 'vivas have 3 main components: skills, content and conduct'. The 'skills' element is an assessment of the candidate's communication skills and of the skill of discussing and defending their work. The 'content' element refers to the assessment of the thesis, and its authentication and exploration during the viva. Finally, they refer to the 'conduct' – the behaviour of the examiners during the viva, and the interactions between the candidate and the examination panel.

Leonard et al. (2006) were commissioned by the Higher Education Academy to review the literature on the experiences of doctoral research students in the UK and on studies focusing on the viva.

Morley et al. (2002) explored the relationship between doctoral assessment and regulatory and quality assurance procedures. They found that, while attempts were being made to ensure quality and consistency within doctoral assessment processes, considerable variation persisted. Carter and Whittaker (2009) argued that the individual nature of the PhD means that the process of examining a doctoral thesis 'remains challenging and is surrounded by different agendas, ideologies and practices'. Tinkler and Jackson (2000) attempted to shed some light on the PhD examination process and focused upon institutional policy from a sample of 20 British universities. Their research revealed some consistency across institutions in terms of their regulations, but also suggested that the operationalisation of regulations and policies may lead to significant diversity.

Joyner (2003) wrote on the important role that the external examiner plays in the assessment process. Joyner concluded that there are two main characteristics that should be required of any potential external examiner: first, subject expertise in order to judge academic standard and whether or not the work makes a contribution to the subject; and second, 'they should also be mature adults, of enough humanity to ensure that the examination process is a worthwhile and developmental experience for the candidate, irrespective of the outcome.'

Wallace (2003) undertook research into the actual conduct of PhD vivas by analysing the language that successful candidates use to describe their oral examination. This research found that some candidates used the metaphors of sport and competition, while others employed imagery relating to imprisonment and interrogation. Wallace then went on to relate these metaphors to the viva and the examiners themselves, and argued that neither models of sporting competitions or interrogation were appropriate within the context of doctoral assessment. Trafford and Leshem (2002a, 2008) examine the very nature of 'doctoralness' and what is really meant by the scholarly nature of the degree.

Johnson (2005) began to examine doctoral assessment and the oral examination within the context of the professional doctorate. This paper raised points of concern relating to the ability and appropriateness of academic examiners in assessing the practice-led nature of professional doctorate candidates. Pearce (2005) explored the entire PhD assessment process and discussed the procedural and scholarly role of examiners, how they examine a thesis and their relationship to the thesis, candidates and other examiners.

2.8 Regulatory frameworks

Table 2.4 (pp. 28–33) reproduces an extract from one university's PhD regulations and I use this to illustrate the main points. Notes (in *italics*) expand on each aspect of the regulations. These regulations are included purely as an example to illustrate the nature of possible regulations for the assessment and award of the degree of PhD. You must check the regulations from your own university, which will be available on the university website and from the Graduate Research School (or equivalent) office.

2.9 Exercises

▶ Write down, in a single paragraph, the contribution to knowledge that you believe has been made by your PhD study. You may already have done so within your thesis. If you have, try to write it down without looking at your thesis. It is important that you begin to be able to quote your contribution so that, when it comes to your examination, you have an answer to the question: 'What contribution does your thesis make?', which you will almost certainly be asked in some way during your viva. Write it down and leave it for now. We will return to it later. To get you started, Figure 2.4 shows you how one student presented her contribution.

▶ Take your PhD thesis and look at your list of references. Produce a list of the most important references. These should be important in terms of *your* study. Try to keep this list to, say, 10 to 20 references, and make sure that it includes a few very recent references if possible. Find your copy of these papers and start to re-read them in preparation for your viva. If you don't have a copy of any of the papers, request one from your university library.

▶ Make sure that you fully understand the methodological approach you have taken and the specific method or methods that you have used during your PhD. If you are unsure about this, or you don't recognise these terms within your own discipline, discuss this with your supervisor so that you are beginning to be able to clearly discuss the approach that you have taken. I will return to questions about methodology in later chapters.

▶ Think about everything that you have done during your PhD and what this has produced. Write a list of the most positive aspects of your thesis.

My Contribution

There has been little work undertaken to differentiate the distinctive characteristics of Higher Education in Further Education (HE in FE). As Jones (2006) commented: 'there is distinct dearth of academic research focusing on the issue of an HE ethos as it relates to the provision of HE in FE' (p. 2). The critical significance of my research, at this time, is imperative. The aim of government post-Browne, and clearly articulated in the BIS White Paper (2011) 'Students at the Heart of the System' is to establish a new innovative HE sector responsible for an improved student experience. But to improve an experience we must first understand what that experience is. I have in this study identified and delineated the unique features of HE in FE and articulated the experience of HE in FE using a range of methods.

Note: The student has justified her contribution in terms of a need for it, and a gap in the literature

This is the first time an in-depth phenomenological study has been undertaken in the subject. The study indicated that the separation of space, HE from FE, was significant in students' lives.

My research in this study has enabled me to characterise and define the nature of HE in FE in a most unique and distinctive way, outlining the following unique characteristics: diversity, closeness, localness, fulfilment, suffering, belonging and dependency.

Note: She goes on to say specifically what the contribution is

HE in FE has evolved over years, but its inimitable features have never been delineated in this way. The ability to define and then market its distinguishing features will be crucial in the future. HE in FE offers something unique. Through my research I have identified the essential nature of that uniqueness and then categorised it. The ability to define and characterise HE in FE, and distinguish its differences from its university rivals, is imperative if HE in FE is to survive and grow.

Note: She alludes to the impact and implications of the work

Figure 2.4   One student's presentation of her 'contribution to knowledge'

Summary

This chapter has discussed the role and nature of the PhD viva, covering the concept of doctoral standards. The concepts of 'contribution to knowledge', 'criticality' and 'independent thinking' have been discussed. The oral examination process has been reviewed, including some examples of alternative models for the viva. A typical timetable for a PhD viva has been presented, and the pages which follow include a sample regulatory framework for the viva as an example (Table 2.4). The findings and conclusions of recent research into the PhD viva have been briefly reviewed.

Hopefully this has helped you to start to gain an understanding of the strange and mystical process that you are about to undergo and to begin to de-mystify it. The next chapter will discuss the role of the examiners in the viva process

---

Topic: Appointment of examiners

Regulation: The supervisor should make the regulations for the examination of the thesis, including the appointment of examiners, clear to the student. The supervisor is responsible for proposing examiners for the approval of the Research Degrees Committee. The supervisor will propose on the appropriate form the examiners for the candidate's examination to the Research Degrees Committee for approval. The Independent Chair will be selected by the Selection of Examiners panel relating to the area of research. This should normally be done 3 months before the expiry date of the registration period or before the examination is expected to take place, whichever is sooner. The examination may not take place until the examination arrangements have been approved. The Research Degrees Committee will approve the final title of the thesis at the same time as approving the examiners and Independent Chair.

Notes: It is appropriate for you and your supervisor to discuss names of possible external examiners in an informal manner, but the final decision on the examination panel rests with the university. In no circumstances should you approach a potential examiner yourself.

The examination arrangements need to be set up well in advance of the submission of your thesis and the arrangement of your viva. The arrangements will need to be formally approved by the university to ensure that the panel has the right expertise and experience to ensure a fair and rigorous assessment of your thesis.

In this case the panel consists of two examiners, one of whom must be external to the university, and an independent Chair who is there to ensure that procedure is followed and that you are treated and assessed in a fair manner.

Table 2.4   Examples of regulations with notes of explanation

Topic: Composition of the panel
Regulation: A candidate for the degree of PhD will be examined by at least two and normally not more than three examiners. One of these will be an external examiner and one other will be a member of staff of the University and not a member of the supervision team. An Independent Chair will also be appointed to preside over the examination but will not take part in the examination process itself. Where the candidate is on the permanent staff of the University, a second external examiner will be appointed. Examiners will be experienced in research in the general area of the candidate's thesis and, as far as is practicable, have experience as a specialist in the topic(s) to be examined. At least one examiner will have substantial experience, that is, normally three or more previous examinations, of examining PhD candidates. An external examiner will be independent both of the University and of any collaborating establishment and will not have acted previously as the candidate's supervisor. An external examiner will normally not be either a supervisor of another candidate nor an external examiner on a taught course in the same Faculty at the University. Former members of staff of the University will not be approved as external examiners until 3 years after the termination of their employment with the University. The Research Degrees Committee will ensure that the same external examiner does not examine more than twice per year in order that familiarity with the Faculty does not prejudice objective judgement. No candidate for a research degree will act as an examiner. Potential examiners are normally required to declare any personal, financial or professional relationships to the candidate.
Notes: These aspects of the regulations are here to ensure that the examiners are completely independent of you and your research, and so that they can assess you and your thesis in a fair and appropriate manner. The composition of the panel will vary, particularly from country to country. However, there will always be at least one external examiner. For example, in New Zealand, the panel is likely to consist of one external examiner from overseas (i.e. from a country other than New Zealand and Australia) and one external examiner from New Zealand or Australia. The point is that there needs to be independence in the examination process, and this is achieved by always including at least one external examiner as part of the panel.
Topic: Examination process
Regulation: The examination for the degree of PhD will have two stages: firstly the submission and preliminary assessment of the thesis, secondly its defence by oral or approved alternative examination. A candidate will be examined orally on the programme of work and on the field of study in which the programme lies.
Notes: The examination is, in effect, in two parts. First the examiners are required to separately and independently read your thesis and form a preliminary assessment of it. They then come together and discuss the work with you before coming to a final decision as to the outcome of your examination.
Topic: Attendance of the supervisor
Regulation: The supervisor or, if more appropriate, the co-supervisor will, with the candidate's consent, attend the oral examination, but will not participate in the discussion. The supervisor will withdraw prior to the deliberations of the examiners on the outcome of the examination.

Table 2.4 continued overleaf

Notes: It is up to you whether your supervisor accompanies you in the viva. In some universities it is normal for a supervisor to go into the viva room with the candidate. In others this doesn't usually happen. If your supervisor does accompany you during the viva, they are there purely as an observer and should not take part in the proceedings unless the Chair of the panel requests them to do so. This would normally be to clarify a specific point.

Topic: Award of the degree

Regulation: The power to confer the degree rests with the Academic Board of the University. The Research Degrees Committee will review the report(s) and recommendations of the examiners and the Independent Chair and will decide on behalf of the Academic Board the outcome of the examination. The written comments and joint recommendation of the examiners and the Independent Chair will together provide sufficient detailed comments on the scope and quality of the work to enable Research Degrees Committee to satisfy itself that the recommendation chosen is correct.

Notes: It is the university that awards the degree, not the examination panel. The university, of course, relies on the judgement of the examiners, and will normally accept their recommendation. In certain rare circumstances, however, the university may ask the examiners to reconsider their decision or appoint a new examination panel.

Topic: The candidate's responsibilities

Regulation: The submission of the thesis for examination will be at the sole discretion of the candidate. Normally a candidate should seek approval of the supervisor prior to submitting the thesis for examination. However, while a candidate would be unwise to submit the thesis for examination against the advice of the supervisor it is his/her right to do so. Equally, candidates should not assume that a supervisor's agreement to submission guarantees the award of the degree. The supervisor must provide a written indication to the student of whether or not the thesis is of a standard which is reasonably likely to satisfy the examiners for the degree proposed. The supervisor must read the thesis and complete the appropriate form for submission along with the thesis to the Graduate Research School.

Notes: This regulation makes it clear that the responsibility for the work within your thesis rests with you, the candidate. You should, of course, listen to the advice of your supervisor and not submit your thesis until you feel it has reached the correct standard and is ready for examination.

Topic: Arranging the examination

Regulation: The candidate will take no part in the arrangement of the examination and will have no formal contact with the examiners or Independent Chair in relation to the thesis and oral examination between the appointment of the examiners and the oral examination. The candidate will confirm, through the submission of a declaration form, that the thesis has not been previously submitted for a comparable academic award. The candidate will ensure that the format of the thesis is in accordance with the requirements of the University Examination Regulations.

Notes: These are standard conditions in most universities. It is not permissible to use the same work for two academic awards without the permission of the university.

Table 2.4 *continued* Examples of regulations with notes of explanation

Topic: The viva
Regulation: Each examiner will read and examine the thesis and prepare, on the appropriate form, independent preliminary written comments before any oral or alternative form of examination is held. Each examiner will be required to submit these preliminary reports to the Graduate Research School prior to the oral examination.
Notes: *The preparation of these preliminary reports ensures that the examiners come to their own independent view of your work before they come to together and discuss it. The reports form a record of these preliminary views. There are different approaches to who is shown these reports. In some universities they are sent to the Independent Chair of the examination so that he/she can be prepared for any differences of opinion when it comes to the day of the viva. In other universities they will be sent to each examiner so that they come to the viva with knowledge of each other's view. In a small number of universities the reports are sent to the candidate so that he/she understands the views of the examiners prior to meeting them at the viva, and knows, to some extent, what to expect from the questioning.*
Topic: Agreeing an outcome
Regulation: Following the oral examination the examiners will submit, on the appropriate form, a joint report and recommendation relating to the award of the degree, together with the examiners' written comments, to the Graduate Research School Administrator. The written comments and joint recommendation of the examiners and Independent Chair will together provide sufficient detailed comments on the scope and quality of the work to enable the Research Degrees Committee to satisfy itself that the recommendation chosen is correct. The Independent Chair will submit a report to Graduate Research School on the conduct of the examination.
Notes: *After the viva, the examiners must agree on an outcome and document this on the appropriate form.*
Topic: The outcome
Regulation: Where the examiners' recommendations are not unanimous, a separate report and recommendation will be submitted to the Research Degrees Committee by each individual examiner to evidence that a detailed assessment of the thesis has been carried out and to clarify the differences in the judgements made. The recommendations will be made on the appropriate form immediately.
Notes: *This regulation makes allowance for the situation where the examiners cannot agree an outcome; that is, they have different views on the thesis and/or the candidate's performance and on whether the required standard has been met. In practice, this situation happens very rarely.*
Topic: The recommendation
Regulation: Following completion of the examination, the examiners choose one of the following recommendations: (a) Pass – the candidate be awarded the degree of PhD (b) Conditional Pass (Minor corrections) – the candidate be awarded the degree of PhD subject to minor corrections being made to the thesis

Table 2.4 continued overleaf

(c) Conditional Pass (Amendments) – the candidate be awarded the degree of PhD subject to more substantial amendments being made to the thesis

(d) Re-submission for PhD – the candidate is permitted to re-submit for the degree of PhD and be re-examined, with or without an oral examination, within twelve months. One re-examination may be permitted by the Research Degrees Committee

(e) Offer the award of MPhil

(f) No degree awarded

Notes: These are the normal outcomes of a PhD viva. It is very rare for a candidate to pass their PhD without any revisions at all to the thesis. It does, however, happen. The most common outcome is that the candidate is required to make some small changes to the thesis. Some universities provide an option where the examiners feel that the candidate has, in general, reached the standard required for the award of PhD but the thesis still requires some quite major amendments. If the examiners feel that the candidate has not reached the standard, and that more work is needed, they can ask for a re-submission of the thesis, usually allowing one year for this. If the examiners feel that the candidate and the work cannot reach PhD standard then they may recommend the award of a Master's degree, usually MPhil. If they feel that the work is extremely weak, they may recommend that the candidate fail. The latter outcomes are very rare. If the examiners feel that the candidate has not reached the required standard the normal outcome would be to ask for a re-submission. Indeed, some university regulations do not allow the examiners to award an MPhil or to Fail the candidate on the first attempt and will always allow the candidate the chance of a re-submission.

Topic: If the examiners can't agree on a recommendation

Regulation: Where the examiners' recommendations are not unanimous, the Research Degrees Committee may: (a) accept a majority recommendation (provided that the majority recommendation includes at least one external examiner); (b) accept the recommendation of the external examiner; or (c) require the appointment of an additional external examiner.

Notes: This happens very rarely, but will be covered by the regulations of most universities.

Topic: Revisions to the thesis

Regulation:
Minor corrections – Where the examiners are satisfied that the candidate has reached the standard required for the degree, but consider that the thesis requires some minor typing, grammatical or spelling errors or small corrections to the text, they may recommend that the degree be awarded subject to the candidate correcting the commentary to the satisfaction of the internal examiner. The examiners will indicate clearly to the candidate in writing what corrections are required. The corrections to the thesis should be completed by the candidate within 3 months of the approval of the examination decision by the Research Degrees Committee.

Table 2.4 *continued*   Examples of regulations with notes of explanation

Amendments – Where the examiners are satisfied that the candidate has in general reached the standard required for the degree, but consider that the thesis requires more major amendments but not, in the opinion of the examiners, sufficient to require the candidate to revise and re-submit, they may recommend that the degree be awarded subject to the candidate amending the thesis to the satisfaction of the nominated examiner(s). Such amendments may involve a major re-write of sections or significant clarification and amendment of arguments. The examiners will indicate clearly to the candidate in writing what amendments are required. The amendments to the thesis should be completed by the candidate within 6 months of the approval of the examination decision by the Research Degrees Committee.

Notes: In most universities the examination panel can award the degree subject to minor, or in some cases more major, revisions to the thesis. The panel must also agree which examiner (or it may be all examiners) are going to read the revised thesis and check that the candidate has undertaken the revisions as required by the examiners. The examiners are required to set out the necessary revisions required.

3 The Examination Panel

On completion of this chapter you will:

▶ understand the composition of the viva panel
▶ understand the importance of the choice of examiners and feel in a position to discuss this with your supervisors
▶ be prepared to research into the background of your examiners, particularly the external examiner
▶ understand the role your supervisor may take in your viva
▶ understand your own role within the viva

3.1 Chapter overview

This chapter outlines the constitution of the PhD viva panel, including the roles of the examiners (internal and external), the independent Chair, the candidate and the supervisor. The expectations of each player are examined in some detail. The importance of choice of examiners is discussed, and tips on how to investigate the previous research experience of your examiners are given. This chapter also includes some discussion as to whether your supervisor should be present during your viva, how that decision is made and what their role is, if they do attend.

3.2 Composition of the examination panel

Your examination panel will have been set up and approved by your university some months before the actual day of your viva. The panel is likely to consist of:

● one or more external examiners
● an internal examiner
● an independent chair

The regulations of your university will prescribe who can be on the panel, and it is likely that you will know who the panel members are well in advance of your viva.

The internal examiner will normally be a member of staff of your university, someone who is knowledgeable of your subject area but has not been involved in your project. In many countries (but not in the USA), your supervisor is not allowed to be your internal examiner. The external examiner will come from another university and will have been appointed because of their particular expertise in your subject area. Both examiners have been appointed to assess your work and whether you have reached doctoral standard.

The examiners are largely doing the job of assessing your thesis because they are interested in reading your work. It takes a lot of time and effort to examine a PhD thesis and, although the examiners are paid for doing so, the fee is usually a low honorarium, so they are clearly not doing it for the money. The very appropriately titled article: '"It's a PhD, not a Nobel Prize": how experienced examiners assess research theses' (Mullins and Kiley, 2002) cites two main reasons that academics gave for wishing to examine a PhD thesis. First, they said that they did it out of a 'sense of duty'. They saw it as part of the job of being an academic; a duty that was theirs to fulfil. They felt that it was up to them, as part of the academic community within their discipline, to ensure that PhD standards were maintained. They also felt a sense of duty to their students and the students of their colleagues in other universities. One academic was quoted as saying: 'if examiners didn't do it, the whole system wouldn't work'. The second reason was interest in the subject and the work. Examiners saw examining a PhD thesis as a way of reading some new work in their subject area in much greater detail than they would find in a journal article. They were doing it because they felt that they would be interested in the work and that they would learn something themselves from reading the thesis.

The role of the independent chair (I will call them simply 'the Chair' from here on) is quite different from that of the examiners. The Chair is there to support you and the examiners, to make sure that the regulations are followed, that you are treated properly and with respect and generally to make sure that all aspects of the viva are carried out in the correct manner.

An example of the relevant regulation from a UK university is:

An Independent Chair will be present at all *Viva Voce* Examinations. The role of the Independent Chair is to aid the examiners in the discharging of their role by advising them on process and procedures and ensuring that the examination is conducted according to the University regulations for Doctor of Philosophy.

Specifically the role of the Chair is to:

- Aid the examiners in the discharging of their role by advising them on process and procedures and ensuring that the examination is conducted according to the university regulations.
- Act as the first point of contact for the examination team.
- Attend the private meeting with the examiners prior to the oral examination where preliminary comments are discussed, and facilitate that discussion, so that the team comes to an agreed way forward for the questioning within the viva.

- Act as a chairperson during the oral examination, but not as part of the examination.
- Ensure that all the relevant documentation is completed in accordance with the university regulations, and that it is returned to the appropriate central university officer as soon as possible after the examination.
- Ensure that the examination is carried out in a fair and consistent manner, and that all parties (the candidate and the examiners) are treated with respect.

Trafford and Leshem (2002a) studied a single viva in detail, highlighting the positive features of the examination and the role of each player. They were two of the five participants (the candidate, the Chair, two examiners and the supervisor) but do not state which two. They found that the candidate felt in control of the situation, was treated with respect, supported and thus able to defend the thesis in a satisfactory manner. They concluded that the presence of a Chair and the supervisor were important and that they helped the viva be a positive experience for the candidate.

In some universities a member of the Graduate Research School Office, or a senior administrator from the Registry, may attend to observe and take notes, and to advise the examiners and the Chair on any regulatory issues. A small number of universities now record the proceedings of each viva, using either video or audio. The recording is then stored securely and can be used as a record of the viva if an issue, such as an appeal, arises subsequently. In some countries in mainland Europe, the examination team will consist of a panel of four or five members, including a mix of internal and external examiners.

Your examination team will be proposed by your supervisor, and will have to be approved by the university. Figure 3.1 (pp. 38–39) shows a sample form for approval of examination arrangements. The criteria for approval are likely to include: experience of examining at PhD level, qualified to PhD level, subject expertise, recent research and publications, and independence (that is, no conflict of interests). The form in Figure 3.1 contains all of the necessary information to allow a panel to assess the examiners against these criteria.

3.3   Choice of examiners

It is normal for your supervisors to approach potential examiners some months in advance of the submission of your thesis, and certainly in plenty of time to allow arrangements to be made for your viva. It is usual to discuss potential examiners with your supervisor. However, the final selection of the examination panel is made, and approved, by the university (as illustrated in Figure 3.1), and in no circumstances should you approach potential examiners yourself. It may be that several potential examiners are considered and put forward to your department and the university before the final selection is made. Carter (2008) discusses the process of selection and approval of examiners in some detail. Wallace and Marsh (2001) stress the importance of choosing the right examiners: 'It is the behaviour of the examiners, rather than their final decision, which is the key factor in making the viva an affirmative or a destructive experience for the successful candidate'.

An example of the relevant regulation from a UK university is given below:

> It is appropriate for the supervisor to discuss names of possible external examiners with the student, but this discussion should remain confidential and in no circumstances should the student seek to contact possible external examiners. The supervisor is responsible for proposing examiners for the approval of the University Research Degrees Committee.

Joyner (2003) argues that 'the external examiner is the most important arbiter of whether a student's submission earns the research degree'. This is probably true, although in the regulations of many universities the internal and external examiners' views carry almost equal weight. Joyner goes on to propose that there are two main characteristics that are important and are required of any potential external examiner. First, they should be sufficiently knowledgeable of the subject area of the thesis to be able to form a judgement as to whether it is of PhD standard, and second, they should be 'mature adults, of enough humanity to ensure that the examination process is a worthwhile and developmental experience for the candidate, irrespective of the outcome.'

The choice of the examiners is very important, and it is something that, if at all possible, you should spend some time discussing with your supervisor. Your view is important; after all it is you who has spent three or more years researching the topic. This gives you an insight into the subject knowledge which is needed to examine your work. However, you also need to approach this with care. As discussed above, the responsibility for selection and approval of the examiners lies with the university, and not with you. Some universities and some supervisors will welcome a discussion with the student concerning potential examiners. Others may view this as inappropriate, so please do check this with your supervisor.

It is likely that, through your reading, you are aware of the work of some academics that might be suitable to examine your work. Set about putting together a shortlist of a few potential examiners and discuss these with your supervisor.

Clearly it is important that the examiner takes a similar theoretical and methodological slant to your own, and at least, is not opposed to the

Application for approval of Examination Arrangements for the degree of Doctor of Philosophy

Name of Candidate: Ms Melanie Viva

Title of Thesis: An investigation into viva performance in Computer Science PhD theses

An abstract of the candidate's thesis (on a single page) must be attached to this application.

Supervisory Team:

Name	Supervisory Role	Department
Dr A Abbott	First supervisor	Education
Prof B Brown	Co-supervisor	Computer Science

Independent Chair (IC):

Name	Department
Professor C Court	Education

Proposed External Examiner

Name (inc Title)	Institution and address	Number of previous research degree examinations	
		MPhil	PhD
Prof Peter Smith	Faculty of Education, University X	20+	50+

Present Post:	Professor of Education
Qualifications:	BSc, PhD, FHEA

Has the Examiner previously examined a PGR student at this University?	No
I declare that I have no personal, financial or professional relationship to the candidate.	X
Research Interests:	Doctoral study, qualitative research methods

Five most recent relevant publications

Sanders, G, Kuit, J, Smith, P, Fulton, J and Curtis, H. (2011) Identity, reflection and developmental networks as processes in professional doctorate development. Work Based Learning Journal, 2(1).

Smith, P, Curtis, H, Sanders, G, Kuit, J and Fulton, J. (2011) Student perceptions of the professional doctorate. Work Based Learning Journal, 2(1).

Thompson, J, Smith, P and Cooper, B. (2012) An autoethnographic study of the impact of reflection and doctoral study on practice. Work Based Learning e-Journal International, 2(2).

Fulton, J, Kuit, J, Sanders, G and Smith, P. (2012) The Role of the Professional Doctorate in Developing Professional Practice. Journal of Nursing Management.

Fulton, J, Kuit, J, Sanders, G and Smith, P. (2013) The Professional Doctorate, Palgrave.

Figure 3.1   A sample form for approval of PhD examination arrangements

Proposed Internal Examiner			
Name (inc Title)	Dept Address	Number of previous research degree examinations	
Dr Petra Smythe	Computer Science	MPhil	PhD
		1	3

Present Post:	Principal Lecturer in Computing
Qualifications:	BSc, PhD, FBCS, CEng, CITP

Has the Examiner previously examined a PGR student at this University?	No

Research Interests:	Artificial Intelligence, Software Engineering

Five most recent relevant publications:

Hall, L, Irons, A, MacIntyre, J, Sellers, C and Smith, P. (2010). Sunderland Software City: An Innovative Approach to Knowledge Exchange in the North East of England. Journal of Research in Post-Compulsory Education, 15 (3). pp. 317-327.

Hamdan, K, Smith, P and Plekhanova, V. (2012). Leadership and Cultural Issues: Evaluation and Measurement in the Context of Software Development Projects. International Journal of Information and Education Technology, 2(1). pp. 68-76.

Belkhouche, B, Hamdan, K and Smith, P. (2013). The Influence of Leadership and Work Culture on Software Cost Effort. Journal of Software, 8(6), pp. 1353-1367.

Beard, R J, and Smith, P. (2013). Integrated electronic prescribing and robotic dispensing: a case study. SpringerPlus, pp. 1-7.

Beard, R, Karimova, G and Smith, P. (2014). Linking integrated electronic prescribing and robotic dispensing: identifying benefits at ward level. European Journal of Hospital Pharmacy.

Figure 3.1 *continued*   A sample form for approval of PhD examination arrangements

approach you have taken. Similarly, it is not wise to suggest an examiner whose work you have directly criticised, or disproved, within your thesis. You also need to avoid any 'conflict of interest'. Your examiner can not be a close friend, or previous colleague or anyone that you have had a previous formal relationship with (for example, a lecturer from your undergraduate days, someone that you worked for in the past, or someone with whom you have co-authored a paper). If an examiner with whom you have had any form of contact is proposed, you need to discuss this with your supervisor. It is likely that your university will have specific regulations or guidelines to help you with this.

Don't be afraid to suggest a very experienced academic as an examiner. My own experience is that the more practised an examiner is, the more sympathetic and reasonable they may be. Experienced examiners are also experienced supervisors. They understand the hard work that you have done and are more likely to be able to look at things from a student's point of view. This is backed up by the research of Mullins and Kiley (2002), who found that 'experienced examiners want [the candidate] to be awarded the PhD and will go to extraordinary lengths to enable this to happen'. They also concluded that 'experienced examiners should be sought for the examination process, not avoided, because of their high degree of tolerance'.

Morley et al. (2002) discuss how your external examiner can ultimately become someone who publicises your work to other academic colleagues. I have also come across PhD graduates who, over time, begin to work with their external examiner, co-authoring papers. An external examiner may also be someone who you may wish to approach in the future as a referee when you are applying for a new post or for advice when you are working on a paper for publication. All of this makes the choice of examiner very important.

Examiners should be discussed and proposed well in advance of submission of your thesis. It is usual to do so well before you expect to complete, and many universities have regulations that stipulate that approval of examination arrangements must take place at least, for example, 6 months prior to submission.

Professor Simon Leather, who is a very experienced PhD examiner, gives some great advice in his blog entry 'Are PhD examiners really ogres?' (2013):

"Do discuss the choice of external examiner with your supervisor. Most supervisors like to give their students some choice in the matter. You may have a particular preference, but your supervisor will know if they have any particular quirks that may not make them the best choice for your thesis. Once you know who the external is, make sure you include some of his/ her references in your thesis. It may seem petty, but it helps get you off on the right foot."

Professor Leather adds further:

"To date, 46 of my students have been examined and received their PhDs. Most have had minor revisions, a couple had major revisions, and not one has failed. In all cases, they were treated with courtesy and respect, even the candidate who when asked why she had repeated an experiment that had been done twenty years previously, replied that it was because the original experiment was deeply flawed, seemingly unaware that her external examiner was the experimenter in question. I have to admit that I almost gasped out loud, especially as the external in question had, many years before, been my supervisor. He, however, took it in [his] stride, smiled and passed her with minor revisions."

The experienced examiners who were interviewed by Kiley and Mullins (2004) warned against sending theses to inexperienced examiners.

3.4 The external examiner

The external examiner performs a particular role within the examination panel. Traditionally the external examiner has been considered the 'senior examiner'. However, in the regulations of most universities, little distinction is made between the internal and the external examiners. Reference is often limited to the situation where the examiners cannot agree on an account and a statement such as: 'in a case where the examiners cannot agree, the Research Degrees Committee may take the view of the external examiner'. Notwithstanding this, it is often the case that the external examiner is the most experienced examiner, and it is also likely that they have the most expertise in the subject. After all, they have been chosen for that very expertise, which means that it is likely that their knowledge of the candidate's subject area is greater than that of the internal examiner.

Therefore, there is often a sense that the external examiner is 'the real expert' within the examination panel, and treated as such by the rest of the panel. This may mean that they ask the majority of the questions.

My own experiences of external examiners are that, in general, they will:

- be genuinely interested in your work;
- read your thesis thoroughly;
- approach your examination in a professional manner;
- be fair and respectful;
- try to help you do your best during your viva;
- only ask for changes to your thesis if they feel that they are absolutely necessary to raise it to doctoral standard.

3.5 Getting 'to know' your external examiner(s)

"I had prepared well and I had 'researched' my panel members to gain some insights about their own interests."

As discussed above, it is not appropriate to approach your external examiner prior to your viva. What you should do, however, is get to know their work because this can help you prepare for the event. You can do this in several ways:

- Use a searching tool such as Google Scholar or your library databases to find any papers that your examiner has written. Look for those that relate particularly to the topic of your thesis.
- Search to see if your examiner has a web page; this is likely to be linked to the university where they work. If they do have a page (or several) this will give you important information about their research interests. It may even contain links to their CV, a list of their publications, and perhaps even provide links to download copies of some of their papers.

- If they work in, or lead, a research group, that group may also have a website which will provide useful details of the research projects that they are working on, and any PhD students that they are supervising.
- Ask your supervisor. It is likely that they are familiar with the research work of your examiner, and will be able to help you in your search.

After you have done the above, collect together and read the most relevant papers by your examiner. Use these in your preparations for your viva. Ask yourself the following questions:

- How does their research work compare with mine?
- Which methodological approach do they take?
- Which theoretical perspectives do they take?
- Which authors do they refer to?

And, of course:

- What questions are they likely to ask?

It is usually not possible to predict with any certainty the questions that the examiners will ask you on the day. In some universities, however, the candidates are given an indication of some of the topics to be discussed. For example, I am aware of one university in the UK which provides PhD candidates with the preliminary report forms of the examiners, so that the candidate is aware of the areas and issues which the examiners wish to explore during the viva. There may well be more. I am also aware of a university in New Zealand that has recently moved to a similar system, and its regulations state that '[c]andidates' preparation for an oral examination or thesis revision should be assisted by knowing what the examiners have said about their thesis.'

However, in many universities the candidate is not provided with any indication of the areas to be discussed during the viva. However, by doing some background research on your external examiner you should be able to get an idea of the perspective that they are likely to take on your thesis and how they might view your work. Discuss this with your supervisor and use this knowledge to help you frame some possible viva questions, which you can then use in your preparations.

It is possible that this exercise will reveal some work that, in hindsight, you wish you had referred to in your thesis. This often happens, and you shouldn't worry about it. Of course, if your examiners have been selected well in advance of the submission of your thesis, you may still have time to do this, and can refer to their work within your own.

I recall very well one of my first experiences as a nervous supervisor, as I collected the external examiner from the station. It was the day of the viva for one of my first PhD students. I knew that the student had done a lot of good work; he had developed a new method, albeit in its early prototype stages, and had already had a paper published in a very respectable journal. I was pretty confident that the student would do well and, as long as he performed adequately during the viva, I fully expected him to be awarded his PhD.

The external examiner we had chosen was very eminent indeed; in fact he was a leading figure in the subject of the student's thesis. I nervously met him off his train, helped him with his bag, and gave him a lift to the university for the viva. One of the first things he said to me was:

> "I really enjoy vivas. I like to put the student through their paces. My own viva was 6 hours long, I really suffered, and I felt I earned my PhD. So I like to make sure all the students I examine feel they have had a good going over."

This worried me. Was he going to subject my student to a gruelling 6-hour viva, and make sure that he too 'suffered' as the examiner had in his own viva? As it happened, the viva was between 2 and 3 hours and my student passed with some quite minor corrections to his thesis. The examiner asked probing questions and made sure that the viva was testing, challenging and rigorous, but it was by no means unfair.

3.6 Should your supervisor be present?

In many universities it is normal for your supervisor to accompany you at your examination. This is your choice, and if the supervisor does accompany you, they will do so as an observer; that is, they are not allowed to take part in the discussion. They are simply there to give you moral support, to observe the proceedings and to take notes. This can be very useful as you will be too busy answering the questions (and possibly too nervous) to make your own notes. Such notes can be really useful later, when you are addressing any issues raised by the examiners, as they can help you to identify exactly where in your thesis the issue arose; this will help to clarify the point the examiners were trying to make.

If your supervisor is not available, it may be possible for you to bring an advisor or co-supervisor to the viva with you. I have even chaired a viva where the candidate brought two supervisors into the examination. This is not normal in the UK system, and would usually only be allowed with the permission of the Chair. The approach taken in some countries is different, and may allow you to bring more than one supporter into the viva with you. For example, in New Zealand, candidates can invite one or two supporters to come into the viva. This began in the recognition that Maori people are not used to being alone in such situations. They would consider it normal to have someone – usually an elder – who will do appropriate prayers and make some supportive comments on behalf of the candidate. So it has been extended to all. This option is apparently not used very often, but is available to candidates. It is worth checking the situation within your own university system.

I know that some students feel nervous about answering questions in front of their supervisor, and have come across a few students who didn't wish their supervisor to accompany them for that reason. However, overall I think it is a good idea for your supervisor to attend; so, if this is possible, I would encourage you to ask your supervisor to accompany you. It can help a lot when it comes to making any revisions to your thesis. Grabbe (2003) argues that supervisors should always attend the viva.

3.7 Your own role in the examination

"You are the expert, and you can relish the opportunity to demonstrate your expertise to a group of interested peers."

It would be remiss of me if I didn't discuss your own role within the viva. After all, it is your examination and you are the most important person in the room. The event has been scheduled to discuss your work; something that you have spent years working towards. The examiners have come to your university to discuss your work with you. They have read your thesis, are knowledgeable in the subject area, and are genuinely interested in what you have done and want to hear what you have to say. So you need to prepare as much as you can to be sure that you do yourself justice. But you also need to be proud of your work and positive about your achievements, and you should enjoy the event.

3.8 Exercises

The exercises which I am presenting here depend upon which stage you are in the examination process.

> ▶ If you are in the final year of your PhD, and the examiners have not yet been appointed, now might be the time to broach the subject with your supervisor. If your supervisor is willing to do so, prepare a list of possible examiners, with reasons as to why they might be suitable examiners for your thesis, and discuss this with your supervisor.

▶ If your examination panel has been appointed, now is the time to begin to research the background of your examiners. Follow the steps outlined in Section 3.5 to find out as much as you can about the research interests and experience of your examiners. Get some of their papers and begin to read them. Make some notes about their interests and start to think about possible questions they may ask you, and which aspects of your thesis they may be particularly interested in. Of course, it is not possible to predict what they will actually ask you during your viva, but you can prepare yourself for some of the possible areas of questioning.

▶ Consider the subject of whether your supervisor should accompany you during the viva. Discuss this with your supervisor. My own personal view is that, if at all possible, you should ask your supervisor to accompany you in the viva.

Summary

This chapter has covered the composition of the viva panel and the importance of the choice of examiners. It has also covered the basis on which examiners are appointed, and explained why you should get to know the research interests of your examiners so that you can use this knowledge to inform your viva preparations. The role which your supervisor takes in the viva has also been discussed, as has your own role. In the next chapter you will begin to examine and plan your viva preparations in much more detail.

4 Preparing For Your Viva

On completion of this chapter you will:

▶ be able to really start preparing for your viva
▶ understand how you can write your thesis with the viva in mind
▶ be reading and re-reading your thesis and the literature that you have covered during your PhD
▶ be able, if required, to design a presentation based on your thesis
▶ understand the nature of a mock viva
▶ have a number of practical exercises to do as preparation for your viva

4.1 Chapter overview

This chapter contains some tips on how and when to start preparing for your viva. This includes tips on writing the thesis with the viva in mind, preparing for your viva in the months before and as the event draws closer, in the weeks and days before. I include some advice on reviewing your work: how and when to re-read your thesis, defining and explaining the contribution made, the literature reviewed and the methodological approach taken. Differences between disciplines are covered, including the possibility of preparing a formal presentation, which is becoming the norm in some subjects. The custom of having a practice or 'mock' viva is discussed, as is the importance of presenting your work throughout the PhD process in seminars, conferences and so on. The chapter makes use of case study material drawn from students, and how they prepared for their own viva. Practical tips, such as preparing chapter summaries and summaries of papers that you have read during your PhD, are given. The issues of student well-being and how to prepare emotionally and physically for your viva are also covered.

> "On reflection I began the preparation for my viva I suppose from the outset of the programme."

The more you prepare for your viva, the more confident you will become. If you are well-prepared there is no reason to fear the experience. All of my own students have been worried about their viva; it is an exam, after all. But they have all actually *enjoyed* the experience. The viva is one of very few occasions in your life when you will get the chance to talk to a group of people who have read some of your work in detail, and who are interested in finding out more about what you have done. It is your opportunity to demonstrate your contribution to a group of other experts who work in a similar field to your own, and to exude your passion in your subject.

"I thoroughly enjoyed every second of the viva."

4.2 Writing your thesis with your viva in mind

When you started your PhD all those years ago, the viva seemed so far in the future that you hardly gave it any thought. As time progressed, and the end drew closer, I'm sure you will have begun to think about and plan for the day that you are sitting in front of your examiners. You should really start preparing for your examination from your very first day, and of course you do, simply by doing your research and starting to write. Trafford and Leshem (2002b) call the small steps you make 'stepping stones'. One of the most important things that you can do during your doctorate is to write. You should begin writing from the very start, taking notes of the research work you do, and writing reports for your supervisor. Soon you will be writing chapters of your thesis. Writing is important for a number of reasons: it helps you to clarify your thoughts, it enables you to present your ideas to others, it can form the basis of discussions with your supervisor, and it lays the foundations for your thesis. It is also important to practise the art of academic writing, which is probably very different from any writing which you have done it the past, and is something which your examiners will assess when they read your thesis. Do some writing every day. The practice will be good, and the academic style will soon become a habit that will start to help you in your research.

The focus of this book is on the viva. There are many books (Dunleavy, 2003; Murray, 2011) devoted to writing your thesis, which give very full guidance and tips on the process. The advice I would give here is that you should produce regular draft chapters of your thesis and give these to your supervisor for review, allowing plenty of time for them to read your work and give you feedback on it. You will then need time to revise the work; drafting, reading, reviewing and redrafting should become a continuous process throughout your PhD. In this way you will refine each chapter of your thesis, allowing plenty of time for final review when you are approaching the end of your studies.

It is important that your thesis is presented to the examiners in as professional manner as possible. This includes your style of writing, the format and presentation (be sure to follow the guidelines provided by your university) and your use of tables, figures and references. The more time you spend on revising and perfecting these aspects of your thesis, the better your final submission will be.

In Chapter 2, we covered doctoral standards and the important characteristics of a doctorate. In Table 4.1, I have adapted Table 2.1 to indicate how you might focus on these areas when you are writing your thesis.

Area	Standard
Contribution to knowledge	The fundamental requirement of the doctorate is that it will lead to the creation and interpretation of new knowledge. *It is essential that your contribution to knowledge comes through clearly in your thesis. Have a section somewhere in your thesis, perhaps in the final chapter which is headed 'Contribution to Knowledge' and make sure that it sets out in concise and precise terms what your contribution is. This will make it easy for your examiners to find and assess the contribution. I have read many theses in which the candidate has not made this clear, and I have had to find the contribution myself, which is not a good start for an examiner. Make it very clear; help your examiners to do their job. A page or so is probably sufficient.*
Grasp of the subject	The candidate should be able to demonstrate a deep understanding of the body of knowledge relating to their topic. *This is referring to your grasp of the literature, and how you demonstrate this within your thesis. You will have one or more early thesis chapters where you review the literature. Your thesis should also include reference to the literature throughout, where you continually evidence what you have done and why through the literature, and compare your results to the published work of others. Your thesis will have a lengthy reference list, or bibliography, at the end. You must ensure that every paper that you refer to within the body of the text is properly referenced in that list, using the referencing style recommended by your university. Many students make small mistakes in referencing. Be consistent. Examiners will pick up on referencing errors and you will be required to correct them. Holbrook et al. (2007) analysed the reports from 501 PhD candidates across five Australian universities. They found that, on average, in about one-tenth of those cases the examiners commented upon the candidate's use of the literature in the thesis. This included coverage (whether the candidate covered enough literature of the main authors, and whether it was up to date), errors in use (missing references, references not in standard format) and the nature of the use of the literature (whether the candidate had really used, and engaged with, the literature in a critical manner).*
Independent researcher	The candidate should be able to demonstrate that they can operate as an independent researcher. *Part of the test of this will come in your viva. One thing that you can do within the thesis is to be careful of using the word 'we', as this may indicate that some of your work has been done with others. If some of your work is collaborative and it has been done within the context of a team project, you need to be very clear about which work is your own, and how it relates to the work of others.*

Table 4.1   Relating your thesis to doctoral standards

Area	Standard
Research methodology	A detailed understanding of applicable techniques for research, and the ability to apply these in a systematic and rigorous manner.
	You should explain, and justify, the methodological approach that you have taken, and describe in some detail how you actually did things. Include discussion of ethical issues and approval. Discuss the limitations of your work. Make sure that you set out very clearly the aims of your work and/or the research questions that you have addressed. Return to these at the end of your thesis and evaluate the final outcome of your work, returning to your aim and research questions.
Critical thinking	The candidate needs to be able to show that they can think and write critically.
	This comes down to what is known as academic writing, where you not only refer to the literature, but really use it, by discussing, reviewing, synthesising and evaluating what you have read. Your thesis should show that you have a deep understanding of what you have read, and how your own work relates to it.
Communication skills	A doctoral candidate must be able to demonstrate that he or she is able to communicate their findings verbally and through their written work.
	Your examiners will use your thesis to assess your writing and presentation skills. A well-presented thesis must be free of typographical and grammatical errors. The presentation should be consistent in terms of the use of headings, the labelling of diagrams and figures, and so on. This takes time, so be sure to leave yourself plenty of space for the final production of your thesis. There is nothing more frustrating for an examiner than to be sent a thesis which is riddled with small errors. It gives a poor impression from the start. The examiners will ask themselves: 'If this candidate can make mistakes in the thesis, how rigorous have they been in their research?'
Substantial project	A PhD is awarded for a substantial piece of work which results in the production of a thesis which is normally in the order of 40,000 to 80,000 words.
	Be sure to stick to the word limit; make sure that your thesis is neither too short nor too long. It must be properly structured with a well-written abstract and a good contents list (check page numbering matches the actual pages in your thesis; I have seen lots where it didn't). Each chapter should start off by introducing its purpose. It should close by explaining what has been covered and what its importance is in the context of your entire thesis, then lead into the next chapter. In some countries the expected word length can be up to 100,000 words.

4.3 Reviewing your thesis

"You will know your work inside out, dear me you've spent three, four or even five years working on it."

One of the best ways to prepare is simply to be fully familiar with what you have written in your thesis. There can often be quite a long time between when you submit your thesis and when you are examined. You are unlikely to forget what you have done, but you may forget how your thesis is organised, or indeed your thinking behind certain arguments. So, you must read your thesis thoroughly several times in the period running up to your viva. Remind yourself of the rationale behind why you did the things you did. In this way you will become better prepared to explain and defend your work during your viva.

You may find it difficult to start reading your thesis again. I know when I have completed a large piece of written work it feels scary to return to it. I guess I am scared in case I find some mistakes, or even something that I no longer like or agree with. Don't worry. This may happen. Students often find mistakes in their thesis. No matter how many times you read, check and re-read your work, some typos seem to slip through. Simply compile a list of these so that, if necessary you can explain to the examiners that you have already found some small errors in your thesis. You may come across something you no longer agree with, because your thinking has moved on since you wrote your thesis. Again, this is not a problem; as long as you can, if necessary, explain why you held that particular position at the time of writing the thesis.

Go through your thesis and start to mark it up so that you can easily find chapters and sections within the document. Your examiners will not expect you to remember every word in your thesis, but you will be expected to discuss exactly what you have done. This will involve referring to your thesis during the examination. It is much better if you can locate sections of your thesis easily, so you don't need to flick back and forth to find a specific section. You will already have a good idea of where things are in your thesis, but it can be useful to use sticky notes to mark specific sections and the start of chapters (see Figure 4.1).

It is also useful to produce a chapter-by-chapter summary of your thesis and type it up on a single page. This will help you remind yourself what appears in each chapter of your thesis. A sample thesis chapter summary is shown in Figure 4.2 (p. 52).

You will be allowed to take notes into the viva. If it makes you feel more comfortable – for instance, taking your chapter summary into the viva with you – it will be acceptable for you to do so. My own experience is that students often take notes and other supporting material into the viva, but in

Figure 4.1   Mark up your thesis using sticky notes

most cases they find that they don't need them and don't use them. However, it helps their confidence by doing so.

4.4 Reviewing the literature

In the exercises in Chapter 2, I asked you to produce a list of your most important references, to get the papers and to start to re-read them in preparation for your viva. You should continue to do so, making notes about the importance of each paper. You will have read many papers during your study, and the reference list in your thesis will consist of perhaps 100 or more articles. You need to focus on those which are most important.

One way of doing this is by producing a table which lists the most important papers, summarises them and says why they are important in the context of your thesis. An example of such a summary is shown in Figure 4.3. Please note that this is included purely as an illustration of how you might prepare such as summary. The two papers in Figure 4.3 are from very different areas (one is computer science and one is education) and it is unlikely that they would figure within the same PhD thesis!

It is, of course, important to continue to read the literature up until your viva. Your examiners will expect you to keep up to date with what is going on in your subject. Your reading shouldn't stop when you submit your thesis.

Chapter One: Introduction
starts on page 6; outlines the rationale for undertaking the research, and motivation for the study; describes the context and background to the study; community-based centres introduced as potential solutions; justified by literature; research aims and objectives presented, along with main research question and hypotheses; brief outline of the methodology used; description of the main project phases; outline of the significance of the project; overview of rest of thesis

Chapter Two: Literature Review
starts on page 21; provides a review of the literature relevant; focused around the central issues of community IT centres, success, sustainability and community participation; the ICT Development Index (IDI) is introduced (page 35); Harris' model for Telecentre Success (2001) is discussed (page 42) as a possible basis for my work; gaps in the literature are identified to underpin my work

Chapter Three: Methodology
starts on page 56; justifies the research paradigm, strategy and methods, specifically the mixed methods methodology; discusses the use of qualitative and quantitative approaches; data collection methods used; use of semi-structured interviews; analysis of existing data; survey of local communities to identify potential barriers to community participation and use of telecentres, based upon a questionnaire

Chapter Four: Data Collection Instruments and Approaches
starts on page 78; presents the design, development and testing of the data collection instruments; the research design for the project is divided into three distinct phases: (1) semi-structured interviews; (2) a questionnaire; (3) the use of a secondary data source; choice of sample, ethical issues and limitations

Chapter Five: The Initial Model
starts on page 92; introduces the initial model on which the study is based; techniques for the development and testing of the model are discussed.

Chapter Six: Results
starts on page 103; presents the results of the three phases of the study; results from phase 1 interviews, the use of thematic content analysis to extract major themes; results from phase 2 survey, the use of simple statistics to present the data; results from phase 3 national survey, utilising simple statistics to present the results

Chapter 7: Discussion and Formulation of Model
starts on page 142; presents a detailed analysis and discussion of the quantitative and qualitative data; synthesises the themes; formulates a new model based on the initial model, and on the previous published model of Harris (2001)

Chapter 8: Evaluation
starts on page 175; evaluates the model with respect to published models (e.g. in particular Harris, 2001); returns to the literature to compare with work of others; discusses limitations; discusses practical implications; returns to aims, objectives and research questions; includes an evaluation by workers in the field

Chapter 9: Conclusion
starts on page 192; presents final conclusions; presents contribution to knowledge; reflects on project and what I have learned; identifies area for future work

References
start on page 198; 175 references cited; have identified 22 key references

Figure 4.2 A thesis chapter summary

Paper 1	
Reference	Hung, C., Wermter, S., & Smith, P. (2004). Hybrid neural document clustering using guided self-organization and wordnet. *Intelligent Systems*, IEEE, 19(2), 68-77.
Abstract	Document clustering is text processing that groups documents with similar concepts. It's usually considered an unsupervised learning approach because there's no teacher to guide the training process, and topical information is often assumed to be unavailable. A guided approach to document clustering that integrates linguistic top-down knowledge from WordNet into text vector representations based on the extended significance vector weighting technique improves both classification accuracy and average quantization error. In our guided self-organization approach we integrate topical and semantic information from WordNet. Because a document-training set with pre-classified information implies relationships between a word and its preference class, we propose a novel document vector representation approach to extract these relationships for document clustering. Furthermore, merging statistical methods, competitive neural models, and semantic relationships from symbolic WordNet, our hybrid learning approach is robust and scales up to a real-world task of clustering 100,000 news documents.
Keywords	neural networks, document clustering, information retrieval
Relevance	This paper presents a model which is quite similar to my own. However they have used a different neural network architecture, and the application domain is information retrieval, which is, again, different from my own.

Paper 2	
Reference	Smith, P., Curtis, H., Sanders, G., Kuit. & Fulton, J. (2011). Student perceptions of the professional doctorate. *Work Based Learning Journal*, 2(1).
Abstract	This paper explores the expectations which students and employers have of a professional doctorate programme. We present a mixed method study of more than 50 students on a professional doctorate programme at a UK university. We explore four themes which have emerged from the study: cohort experience; structure and academic support; personal impact; and employer perceptions. We critically assess these findings against other published studies, and draw conclusions which we believe are of use in the future development of professional doctorate programmes.
Keywords	professional doctorate, student perceptions, employer perceptions, cohort experience, academic support, personal impact
Relevance	This paper explores student expectations of a professional doctorate programme. This is useful and relevant to my own study; however the doctoral programme which the authors have based their study on is very different to the PhD student programmes which I am studying

Figure 4.3 Summaries of two papers

4.5 Preparing for the day

"I found the lead up to the viva quite stressful. Having run a successful business for 13 years I was not prepared to find this a daunting experience, but as the time moved closer, it began to feel like an interview which was not only for a job but a judgement of my life. My supervisor was supportive, reminding me of my journey and getting me to consider how far I had come ... The viva was not only a defence of my work, ... [but] a judgement of the choices I had made, and me!!!!"

As the day of your viva approaches you should make every possible preparation to ensure that everything is in place for it to run smoothly. Read all of the guidance and any other documents that your university provides concerning your viva. Making sure that you understand everything about the format of the viva, your panel and the process will help you to feel confident. In the next sections, I give some advice on what you might do the night before and on the day of your viva.

4.5.1 The night before

Your planning should continue up to the day of your viva, including the night before. Making sure that everything is in place will help you approach your viva day in a calm and confident manner. As I have continued to stress throughout this book, you should be confident, positive and proud about the work you have done. You should be looking forward to your viva; you really are on the final lap. You will have read and re-read your thesis, so it is probably not a good idea to do so again the night before the viva. Concentrate on the practicalities of getting a good night's sleep and planning to ensure that you will arrive at your viva in good time.

Ensure that you eat well with a healthy and balanced evening meal, and go to bed early to ensure that you have a good night's sleep. Think about how you prepared for undergraduate examinations. Oh, and if that involved going for a drink the night before your finals, forget about doing that again. I remember going to see Ian Dury and the Blockheads the night before one of my final exams at school, and not getting home until well after midnight. I did pass the exam, but I was pretty tired on the day and I'm sure that I didn't do my best. I wouldn't do it again. After all, the viva is an examination, and you need to treat it seriously.

Get organised for the next day. Ensure that you have collected everything you need for your viva so that you can easily find it in the morning. Double-check the time and location of your viva. Think about how you are getting to the room, and check the bus or train times. Briefly review your notes for the day if you wish, but you shouldn't spend too much time doing so because you will already have looked through several times during your preparations. The night before is the time to sort out the practicalities of the next day; so that you feel confident and in control.

4.5.2   The day of your viva

Aim to arrive at least 15 to 30 minutes early for your viva. This will give you plenty of time to meet your supervisor, find the room and settle down before your examination actually starts.

Don't forget to take your thesis with you! That might sound silly and obvious, but I have attended at least one viva when the candidate didn't bring a copy. You will not be expected to have memorised everything in your thesis, but you are expected to know and understand what you have done, and be able to discuss this with the examiners. This will almost certainly involve referring to your thesis during the examination. It is much better if you can locate sections of your thesis easily, so you don't need to flick through to find a specific section. You will already have a good idea of where things are in your thesis, but it will be useful to mark it up with sticky notes, as discussed earlier in this chapter. It's also a good idea to take a notepad and pen so that you can make a note of any comments that are made at the end of the examination, and any revisions that you may need to make to your thesis. It is also acceptable to take notes or documents into the viva with you.

Don't forget about your appearance on the day. You should be smartly, but comfortably, dressed; wearing anything that is too informal can suggest that you aren't taking your viva seriously. I have been asked in the past by candidates how they should address their viva panel. In general, it is best to be formal, and address the Chair and examiners as Dr or Professor.

Be positive and confident, and don't worry.

"I saw the viva as an opportunity to showcase my work and speak with people who are interested in the work I had undertaken."

"I certainly did not find it intimidating or challenging but an intellectual conversation that stretched me, but which I actually enjoyed."

4.5.3   A formal presentation?

In some countries and some UK universities, there is a requirement for PhD candidates to make a formal presentation of their work at the start of the viva. This seems to be becoming commonplace in subjects such as computer science and engineering. If you are considering preparing a presentation for the examiners, and it is not a formal requirement, you must discuss this with your supervisor because it may be necessary to gain the agreement of the Chair and the examiners of your viva panel.

Your presentation will normally be prepared using a presentation software package such as Microsoft® PowerPoint, and will be expected to be relatively short; usually no more than 20 minutes. If you are required to make such a presentation you will be informed about the requirements and the time constraints.

Your presentation should cover, as a minimum, the following:

- A title slide, introducing the presentation
- Your aim(s) or research questions
- A brief summary of the literature you have covered and how it underpins your project
- Your methodological approach
- What you have done – a small number of slides giving an overview of your work
- Results
- Evaluation; limitations
- Contribution
- Future work

It is important that you stick to the time limit and that you practise (and time) your presentation before the day. Keeping to the point and keeping on time are important skills. You should prepare your presentation well in advance, and discuss it with your supervisor.

Your presentation should be structured in a logical manner, and provide a critical and evaluative summary of your work and the main findings. You should design it so that it provides a natural starting point for the examiners' questions. The point of the presentation is to explain your work and your contribution, and to show that you can reflect on your findings. It is not a test of how well you can make a presentation, so don't include animations or any gimmicks (unless that is the subject of your thesis). An outline of a presentation is shown in Figure 4.4. Doing a presentation can be a good idea; it will help you to structure your thoughts and can enable you to cover some of the areas that the examiners are likely to ask, putting you a little more in control of the structure and flow of your viva.

If you are studying in a country where the viva is a public event, there will almost certainly be a requirement to make a presentation. This will be to a public audience, and may be expected to be a longer presentation than discussed above. It is likely that, in these circumstances, the viva will be in two parts: a public element where you make your presentation to a large group, followed by a private element where you are questioned by the examiners.

If you are making a presentation; have it loaded on a memory stick. You would be well-advised to load your presentation onto the computer in the viva room the day before the viva. You should run through the presentation on the actual computer in the actual room if at all possible. Then you will be sure that it will run and display exactly as you expect.

Slide 1: Introduction
Thesis title Your name

Slide 2: Aim and Questions
Set out your aims/research questions These should appear exactly as they do in your thesis, using the same words These may appear here or could come after the Motivation and Literature review slides

Slide 3: Motivation
Why the study is needed Justify your study in terms of the literature Explain the background to your work

Slide 4: Literature Review
Give an overview of the relevant literature Highlight key authors and papers Explain why your study is needed; what is the gap in the literature? How does the literature underpin your work?

Slide 5: Methodology
Explain your methodological approach Why did you choose this particular approach over others? Present the methods that you have used in your study Mention any ethical issues Highlight the limitations of your approach

Slides 6 and 7: Your Study
Take a couple of slides to explain exactly what you have done Use diagrams if possible

Slide 8: Results
Present your main results Discuss what these mean Relate your results back to the literature How did you evaluate your work? How does it compare with the work of others in the field?

Slide 9: Conclusions
Discuss your main conclusions Highlight areas for future work What are the implications of your work?

Slide 10: Contribution
The contribution is so important it warrants a slide of its own You may wish to end with this, or be up front and include it as one of your first slides

Figure 4.4 An outline of a short PhD viva presentation in 10 slides

Note: A presentation of this nature should take 10 to 15 minutes, which (unless you are required otherwise) is the sort of length of presentation which most examiners would welcome. You must, of course, practise and time your presentation so that you don't run over time on the day of your viva.

4.5.4   Practice-based PhD: exhibition or performance?

In some practice-based PhD programmes, particularly in the arts and in some professional doctorate programmes, the candidate may be expected to display their work or perform prior to the viva. For example, it may be that the submission takes the form of a thesis accompanied by artefacts such as pieces of art, or examples of the candidate's practice. If this is the case, the first part of the viva may take the form of a discussion of the candidate's practical work.

I have attended and chaired a number of vivas in art, where the student has created a range of work, for example glass sculpture, during their PhD studies. The thesis discusses the work, the candidate's practice and the technical processes of producing the work. It also relates it to theory and the work of others, and draws out the contribution. The viva is often located within, or adjacent to, a gallery where the candidate's work is displayed. The first part of the viva is a tour of the work, during which the candidate presents the pieces to the examiners, discusses them and answers any questions which the examiners may have. The viva then proceeds as normal with the examiners, Chair and candidate sitting down around a table for a question-and-answer session.

If your PhD and viva are of this nature, take great care in selecting the artefacts that you intend to display and present. If you have a lot of work, it may be better to select a limited number of pieces which demonstrate the main points of your thesis. Alternatively, you may wish to select artefacts which demonstrate the chronology of your work or the techniques used. Whichever you choose, there needs to be a clear logical thought process behind your choice which relates the artefacts to the arguments you have presented within your thesis. You need to show that you have exercised criticality in choosing the pieces to show to the examiners. I remember attending one viva where the candidate had simply displayed all of their work. In one sense, this was impressive because it was a very considerable body of work. However, the examiners then asked the candidate to choose the five most important pieces and discuss why they were the most relevant and important in relation to the arguments which were being presented within the thesis.

If you need to make such a presentation as part of your viva, think about how best you can relate the demonstration of your practice to your thesis, and discuss this with your supervisor before making the final choice.

4.5.5   Learning outcomes

Certain doctoral programmes require the candidate to provide evidence that they have achieved the learning outcomes of the programme. This is often

Programme Learning Outcome	Where evidenced in thesis	Where evidenced in portfolio of evidence
K1. Deep understanding of the recent developments in their profession nationally and internationally	2.1 Policy Literature 8.1 Conclusions for the Sector 8.2 Impact and Contribution to Practice 8.3 Personal Reflections	Section 11 Wider Contribution: LSIS Lead provider case study; LSIS Peer Exchange Group Section 12 Dissemination: Articles in Times; Article in Update
K2. Deep understanding of current theoretical frameworks and approaches which have direct relevance to their own professional context	2.1 Policy Literature 2.2 Academic Literature 2.3 Summary 8.1 Conclusions for the Sector 8.2 Impact and Contribution to Practice 8.3 Personal Reflections	Section 11 Wider Contribution: LSIS Lead provider case study; LSIS Peer Exchange Group Section 12 Dissemination: Articles in Times; Article in Update
S1. Make a significant contribution to practice within their chosen field	Chapter 6 Quantitative and Qualitative Findings	Section 7 The Queens Award Section 8 Replica Projects; Move On report Section 11 Wider Contribution: LSIS Lead provider case study; LSIS Peer Exchange Group Section 12 Dissemination
S2. Apply theory and research methods within the workplace, and feel comfortable in integrating different approaches to address 'messy' multidisciplinary problems in a rigorous yet practical manner	4.1 Overall Approach 4.2 Qualitative Study 4.3 Background 6.3 Qualitative Study 6.3 Impact	Section 14 Empirical Research
S3. Recognise budgetary, political, strategic, ethical and social issues when addressing issues within the workplace	6.3 Impact	Section 3 Test the City Marketing Section 11 Wider Contribution Section 13 Examples of Materials and Assessments: Assessment strategy
S4. Reflect on their own work, and on themselves, and thus operate as a truly reflective independent practitioner	3.1 Early Career Reflections 3.2 English and Maths Curriculum and Early Projects 3.3 Summary Chapter 7 Personal Reflections 8.3 Personal Reflections	Section 12 Dissemination Published paper in journal

Figure 4.5   Demonstration of achievement of learning outcomes by a professional doctorate candidate

the case in Professional Doctorate programmes (Fulton et al., 2013). If this is the case for you, you will need to produce a table or a diagram which shows how you have covered the learning outcomes within your thesis or alternative submission. Figure 4.5 shows how one student demonstrated that she had covered the learning outcomes of her programme. In her case, the submission took the form of a thesis and supporting evidence, presented within a portfolio. Figure 4.5 shows the location of evidence of achievement of the learning outcomes in the candidate's thesis and the accompanying portfolio of evidence in tabular form.

4.6 The mock viva

It is quite common to have a mock, or practice, viva. Each university will approach this in a different way, and the mock viva can thus take several forms:

- a practice examination with your supervisors;
- a discussion with other students;
- an attempt to simulate an examination with academic staff who are not your supervisors.

The mock can take place:

- a few weeks, or even months, before your viva;
- days before the viva;
- before you have submitted your thesis, and thus in time for you to react to feedback in terms of making revisions to the draft thesis.

There are other approaches which are similar to the mock viva. These include:

- videos of staged (or in some cases real) vivas – check with your university as they may well have one for you to watch;
- the use of simulated vivas during research student training programmes which may involve students or staff or both.

There is no agreed standard approach for the mock viva. In some cases you may simply be observing others playing out a viva. This will be useful, but it is also important for you to experience a practice viva in the role of the candidate, so that you can gain some sense of what it feels like to be in that situation. Each university has its own approach and practices. In my own university we ensure that every PhD candidate is offered a mock viva (whether they have one is up to them, although we strongly encourage it), but the exact approach taken is left for the supervisor and the student to decide between them.

The following quote is from a student who is discussing the difference between their mock viva and their actual viva.

"The viva was similar but at the same time totally different from the mock viva. It seemed to focus on a (different) small subset of the work and largely ignored other areas."

It seems that the mock viva attempted to cover all aspects of the work, but in the real viva, the examiners were particularly interested in one aspect of her thesis. This could have been because it was important or interesting, or they may have had some concerns about that area of the work. (It was actually the last of these.) The student passed, but had to make some revisions to the thesis which related to that part of her work.

All of the above are valid and useful approaches. Indeed, I have known some candidates have several mock examinations (for example, one with their supervisors, and one with fellow students). The most important thing, and something that I must stress here, is that the mock is a chance to practise, but should not be seen in any way as a rehearsal for the real thing. It is impossible to predict the questions that your examiners will ask. It is possible to predict some of the general questions that *might* come up, and I do so throughout this book, but no-one can predict the very specific questions that relate directly to your thesis.

Little research has been done on the subject of the mock viva; Hartley and Fox (2004) undertook a study (perhaps the only formal study) on the subject, using a questionnaire to gather data on the experiences and feelings of 29 UK postgraduate students concerning their mock viva. The results confirm that there are many different approaches being used in UK universities. Hartley and Fox also found that candidates are often asked questions during a mock which are very different from the questions which come up during the actual viva. However, 90% of the students in the study felt that having a mock viva was a useful experience.

"A couple of weeks before the date of my examination I had a practice viva with my supervisors asking the types of questions that they felt would come up. This process gave me confidence on the one hand, but also made me realise that I had to really revise and read up on the theoretical concepts underlying my work before the big day. This preparation paid off as indeed several questions on theory did come up."

It is important that mock vivas are treated seriously by both staff and students. They should be prepared for, should include at least two staff playing the role of examiners, and should last for at least one hour (Hartley and Fox, 2004). It is important that candidates are provided with feedback after the mock, on their performance and what they may wish to focus on during preparations for the real viva. In my own experience, mock vivas are quite tricky; it is important to take great care with how they are handled. They should be used to support the student, and it sometimes difficult to get the right balance of rigour and academic critique without, on the one hand, terrifying and frightening the student, or on the other hand, giving the student a false sense of security about their chances in the real viva. Each student reacts differently in a viva situation, and this should be taken into account when deciding which approach to take in each case.

> *"It followed a rigorous almost torturous practice viva a couple of weeks prior during which I learned many lessons. You never know what topics or questions will be raised, however you can prepare your method of response, and practise answering questions."*

Tinkler and Jackson (2004) recommend that you discuss the mock viva with your supervisors and choose a form and style accordingly. You should prepare for a mock viva as you would for the real thing. It is good practice to do so, and it is important that you are prepared for it in order for you to maximise the benefits of the mock. Whichever style of mock you choose, remember that it is all part of the preparations for your real viva, and only one of many things that you will do in the months and weeks before you have your examination.

Jenna Condie (2013) of the University of Salford reflected on her own experiences of a mock viva:

> *"I submitted my PhD thesis just over a month ago. Since handing in, I've been a tad unenthusiastic about looking at it again. When I do read it, the writing seems unfamiliar, almost as if someone else wrote it. If the viva was the day after submitting my thesis, whilst I might be delirious, at least I would still be immersed in my research. As more time passes, I feel increasingly distanced from my work.*
>
> *However, I recently had a mock viva and this has changed everything. In preparation for the real thing, my supervisors organised a practice run with two academics that I didn't know. The mock ran as similar to the real thing as possible. I waited outside whilst the examiners convened. I was called in and we shook hands. They started with some easy questions to get the conversation flowing, which then proceeded into a more intense 'grilling' of the how's and why's of my research. All the while, my supervisor sat quietly taking notes on my performance. It lasted for around two hours and I left the room red faced with a pounding head. They had a chat and I re-entered the room for feedback. Here's a summary of what they said:*
>
> - *Rehearse your answers – so that I convey the main points of my thesis more clearly and concisely. Although I made some good points, I did waffle on at times and strayed from answering the question.*

- *Your language impacts upon perceived confidence – avoid vagueness and saying words such as 'stuff' and ending sentences in 'I think'. I need to find ways around this and further rehearsal of arguments is crucial to giving a confident impression.*
- *It's ok if you can't answer a question – I tried to answer everything. Prepare phrases that give you a get out e.g. 'that was beyond the scope of the study'. It's also ok to ask for clarification e.g. 'could you expand on what you mean'.*
- *Summarise each paragraph of your thesis into a sentence – even though I had my thesis with me, there wasn't time to read over sections in the flow of conversation. One suggestion was to summarise each paragraph into a sentence so that when examiners refer you to a section, you have a condensed version.*
- *You must own it – it is my research, I have done a good job, I need to believe my research and defend what I have produced. It makes an original contribution to knowledge, and what I did met the research aims.*

On reflection, I can see that the distance between the research and I impacted upon my performance in the mock viva. I now have a clearer idea of how to go forward in preparing more thoroughly so I enter the real thing with greater confidence. Having a mock viva also gave me the opportunity to talk about my research with others which has reignited some of the enthusiasm that I used to have for my work oh so long ago now.

I don't understand how someone can go into a PhD viva cold. As it's such an unusual scenario, it requires a rehearsal. I think the mock viva worked so well for me as it ran as close to an actual viva as possible. I wouldn't have taken it as seriously if my supervisors or colleagues had played the role of examiners. The experience has made me feel more positive about my work and given me a number of ways forward. Fingers crossed I get a date for my viva sooner rather than later so I can keep this momentum going."

Jenna has since had her viva, passed and been awarded her PhD.

4.7 Treat your viva as you would any important interview

Consider what you would do if you were going for an important job interview. After all, the viva is an interview; albeit a particular and 'intensive' (Brenner, 1985) form of interview. There are many papers and texts on interviewing techniques (Higham, 1983; Fontana and Frey, 1994).

For a job interview, you would research the role you are applying for and the organisation that you are applying to. Well, you should do exactly the same when it comes to your viva. *For your viva,* find out as much as you can about the viva, the regulations of your own university as they apply to the viva, and about your examiners.

For a job interview, you would think about how well your experience, interests and skills match the requirements of the job and the organisation. *For your viva,* consider how well you match the standards of a doctorate. Make sure that you are clear about your research questions, your contribution, the literature, your methodology and your results, and all of the other aspects that are important for the award of a doctorate.

For a job interview, you would anticipate some of the questions that you think might be asked, and prepare some answers to those questions. *For your viva,* you should think about all the general and specific areas that the examiners might question, and prepare and practise some model answers to those questions.

For a job interview, you would find out what form the interview will take, for example whether it is a single one-to-one discussion, a panel interview or a group discussion. *For your viva,* the requirements and format will be specified by the university. Make sure that you research and understand them.

For a job interview, you would plan the day of the interview, including your journey to the venue with an aim of arriving at least 15 minutes early. The night before you would go to sleep early because we all perform better when fresh and fully alert. *For your viva,* you should do exactly the same.

In other words, *for a job interview,* you would prepare properly, plan and practise. *For your viva,* you should do exactly the same thing.

4.8 Disseminating your work before your viva

In most countries, there is no requirement to publish your work prior to submission of your thesis. If you are able to do so, and if your paper is accepted before your viva, it is a big accomplishment, and something that you will rightly be very proud of. Most examiners are impressed when they receive a thesis and find that the candidate has already published some of their work, particularly if it has been published in a reputable journal.

Dissemination of your work prior to submission can also be seen as an important part of the research training process. Attending and presenting at conferences, in particular, is an excellent preparation for your viva (Dinham and Scott, 2001; Tinkler and Jackson, 2008). It will give you experience of presenting your work to an audience, and explaining and discussing it in a way that other members of your academic community can understand. It will enable you to enter into academic debate with peers, and test your skills of thinking on your feet and performing under pressure; skills which will be tested further during your viva. You will receive immediate feedback on your work and gain experience of answering unexpected questions on the subject matter of your PhD thesis, its content and your methodological approach. So, if you have the opportunity to present your work as a paper or a poster at a conference prior to submission, I would encourage you to do so. A somewhat similar experience can be gained by presenting your work at seminars and during formal reviews of your progress.

If I receive a thesis to examine and I see that the student has published their work in a journal (and particularly if I know that the journal has a policy of rigorous peer review), I will start reading the thesis with an enhanced level of confidence that the work is likely to be of a certain standard. Reputable journals will only publish work which is original and thus, by definition, makes some sort of contribution. I will, of course, read the thesis in as much detail as I would any other thesis, but I will start the process in an especially positive frame of mind.

So, if you are reading this well in advance of completion and have the chance to publish your work, I would encourage you to do so. You must, of course, discuss this with your supervisor and take their advice. There are several other benefits to publishing your work prior to examination. It is an opportunity to practise and further develop your academic writing skills, it will give you some important feedback on your work, and it will also provide some written material which can be revised and reformatted and become part of your final thesis. It also gives you practice of the publication process, which is a vital skill, particularly if you wish to pursue a career in academia. In addition, it enables you to get your work 'into the slipstream of academic ideas, and so avoid your thesis becoming just "shelf-bending" research, sitting in your university library and slowly bending a shelf over the years' (Dunleavy, 2003). There are many good books available on the subject of academic writing, including Craswell's *Writing for Academic Success: A postgraduate guide* (2005), Day and Gastel's *How to Write and Publish a Scientific Paper* (2012), and Murray's *Writing for Academic Journals* (2009).

If you have already submitted your thesis, you should spend some time planning a paper or two and discuss this with your supervisor. Planning and drafting a paper can help you in your viva preparations, while you wait for the day of your exam. Think about which chapters of your thesis could form the basis for a paper. Is it one paper or more? Which journal might you choose to send your work to? During your viva, it will be a positive if you can explain that you are preparing a paper for publication, and an even bigger positive if it has been accepted.

4.9 Well-being

The most important thing you can do in preparing yourself for your viva in terms of emotional well-being is to *believe in yourself* and prepare well. If you make good solid preparations for your viva you will feel more in control of the situation and should perform well on the day. After all, as I have said at several points in this book, you know your work better than anyone else, so there is really no need to worry *too* much about your viva. Of course, it is natural to be concerned about such an important event, but if you prepare well, your worries should be manageable.

Your supervisors, and your university, will give you information about the viva and help to prepare you for it as much as they can. However much they do so, the viva will still remain a somewhat unknown commodity. Murray, in her paper 'Students' questions and their implications for the viva' (2003), discusses how students have 'anxieties, expectations and gaps in their understanding of the viva'. Wellington (2010) reports that students' prior knowledge of the PhD viva comes from a variety of sources, including their supervisor, university handbooks, and websites, and that 'by far the most commonly reported source' is friends who have previously experienced their own viva. Wellington goes on to stress the importance of preparing for the viva.

If you find anything that you don't understand about the process, your thesis or the literature, sitting around getting stressed won't help. Instead, take action to address the problem directly by talking to your supervisor, fellow students or staff within the Graduate Research School office. Don't keep things bottled up. Discuss your viva with friends, family, fellow students and your supervisor. Confiding in someone you trust, and who will be supportive, will help a lot. Keep thinking positive. If you start to worry, think positive thoughts about your viva. Tell yourself: 'I know my work', 'I can do this'. Plan your preparations for your viva and allow plenty of study time. But also allow time for breaks and relaxation. Try to maintain a healthy lifestyle during the time up to your viva. You will worry more if you feel tired and overworked. Make sure you allow time for fun and relaxation so that you avoid burning out, but don't drink too much alcohol. Regular moderate exercise will boost your energy, clear your mind and reduce feelings of stress.

There are many techniques for preparing yourself for exams, including coping strategies. For example, the British Journal of School Nursing (2013) presented a project to reduce pre-exam stress which piloted a self-help programme called STEPS (Strategies to Tackle Exam Pressure and Stress). STEPS included videos of former students talking about how they coped, and the chance for students to practise anxiety management techniques such as deep breathing and 'positive visualisation'. Juniper et al. (2012) describe the development of an assessment to evaluate the well-being of PhD researchers. Their study suggests that the well-being of PhD students depends upon personal development, facilities, home and health, research, social aspects, supervisor support and the university environment. Stubb et al. (2011) surveyed 669 doctoral students in Finland, and found that students felt that engagement with the academic community and the support of peers and supervisors was extremely important to their well-being.

4.10 Exercises

You should now be well on with your viva preparations. As exercises from this chapter, you should do the following activities.

▶ Read and re-read your thesis to be sure that you know it thoroughly. Mark up your thesis with sticky notes at the start of each chapter and important sections to that it is easy to find and refer to them in the viva.

▶ Re-read the summary of your contribution and revise it if necessary.

▶ Keep reading so that you continue to be up to date with the literature. Select the papers that are most important and relevant to your thesis and produce summaries of them.

▶ Ask your supervisor to arrange a mock viva. Ask fellow students and friends and family to question you about your thesis. Try to explain your thesis to family and friends who are not familiar with the subject area.

▶ Read any material or guidelines about the viva which are provided by your university. Make sure that you fully understand everything connected with your viva.

▶ Plan a paper for publication with your supervisor(s).

▶ Produce a detailed preparation plan covering all of the above exercises and those covered within the earlier chapters of this book.

Summary

There are many activities that you can do to help you plan and prepare for your viva, and I have tried to cover these within the chapter. Specifically, these include:

- Writing your thesis with the viva in your mind from the outset.
- Reviewing your thesis and producing chapter summaries.
- Reviewing the literature that you have covered in your PhD studies, deciding which are the most important for your viva, and summarising these (and why they are important).
- Preparing a presentation (if required).
- Preparing to present a practice-based PhD.
- What to do the night before.
- What to do on the day of your viva.
- Tips on emotional and physical well-being.
- The mock viva.

continued overleaf

I would encourage you to have a mock, or practice, viva, but do not have unrealistic expectations about it. The mock viva cannot fully represent the *content* of the real viva. The questions asked in your mock viva will differ from those likely to be asked by the true examination panel, simply because the individuals are different and they will have their own distinct areas of interest that they will ask you about. You must treat it as a practice at answering questions, and as a way of gaining an insight into the viva process.

In the next chapter, I will cover some typical questions that might arise during your viva, and how to prepare for them.

5 Typical Questions and How to Answer Them

On completion of this chapter you will:

▶ have a good idea of the typical sort of questions that you might be asked during your viva
▶ understand the different sort of questioning styles that you might encounter and how to respond
▶ understand how examiners approach an examination and prepare their questions
▶ be able to produce your own list of possible questions to use in your viva preparations

5.1 Chapter overview

In this chapter we'll cover some typical questions that might come up during your viva and how you might approach answering them. Although, as I have stated several times, it is not possible to predict the questions that you will be asked during your viva, there are some areas of questioning which arise in almost every viva. Trafford (2003) observed a number of vivas and recorded examiners' questions, concluding that patterns of generic questions can be discerned and that these transcend disciplines. In this chapter I have attempted, based on my own experience, to construct a list of question areas. The majority of this chapter is devoted to discussing those possible question areas, the sort of questions that might arise in those areas, and how you might respond to them.

5.2 Typical questions

Possible Question Area: The 'opening' question

The examiners will quite often start the viva with an open question; perhaps something like this: 'Spend five or ten minutes telling us about your work, what you have done, and what the contribution is.' or 'Summarise your work for us in a single sentence.' Questions like this give you an opportunity to explain your work up front, break the ice, settle you in and get you talking.

Preparing your answer

You should have a short answer prepared in anticipation of an opening question asking for a five- to ten-minute summary. Your examiners may, of course, choose not to start the viva in this way, but it is quite possible that they will and you need to be prepared for it. Think about what you have achieved, why you did it, how you did it, and what the contribution is. As I have outlined several times, the contribution is one of the most important aspects of the PhD, so you need to be very clear what yours is. Your answer should be to the point and no longer than the examiners' limit. Write it down and practise it before the day of your viva.

The 'Summarise your work for us in a single sentence' question is interesting, and another important exercise for you to try. One of the skills that you will have developed in your PhD is communicating concisely and precisely, both in writing and speaking. A question like this is designed to test that skill. Try to practise this by writing a single sentence which summarises the work that you have done, and what its impact is. You should be able to speak with authority, knowledge and confidence about your work, but without arrogance or being closed to the ideas of others.

Possible Question Area: The motivation for, and purpose of, the work

The examiners may ask about the motivation, or reason, for the work.

Preparing your answer:

There must have been a reason for doing your study. All PhD studies set out with a purpose. Be clear as to the purpose of *your* work. What question were you trying to answer? What issue were you exploring? What problem were you trying to solve? Think about the history of your work, and how you came to study that particular topic. 'Because my supervisor told me to study this' is not a good answer. If that is the truth (that is, the project was already set up for you when you started your PhD) you still need to think about why it was set up, and for what purpose. There must have been a reason for your choice of PhD topic. After all, you, your supervisor and the university all agreed that it was a worthwhile topic of study. Make sure that you can explain and defend the reasoning behind this choice.

Possible Question Area: The aim/objectives/research question/ hypotheses

In your thesis you will have set out the purpose of your work. Depending on the discipline that you working in, you may have called this an aim (with accompanying objectives), a question (or a series of questions) or a hypothesis (or a series of hypotheses). It doesn't matter what you have called this in your thesis; you need to be prepared to explain and justify it to the examiners.

Preparing your answer

I'll refer to an 'aim' here. The aim of your work should be set out in very clear and unambiguous terms. Find it in your thesis and write it down somewhere. If you don't have one in your thesis, write one down now. Look at it carefully, reading each and every word. Be prepared to justify every word and explain why it is there. Have you achieved it? If your research is based on a question, have you answered it? It is likely that it changed as the work went on. This is normal. Be prepared to discuss and explain this to the examiners.

Some candidates I have supervised have found it useful to produce a diagram which gives an image of their questions, and how they relate to each other. Figure 5.1 illustrates how this can be done. In the diagram, the

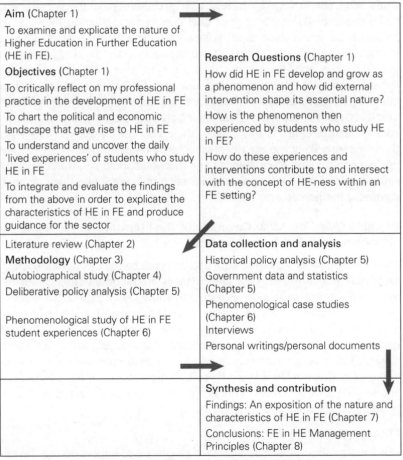

Aim (Chapter 1)

To examine and explicate the nature of Higher Education in Further Education (HE in FE).

Objectives (Chapter 1)

To critically reflect on my professional practice in the development of HE in FE

To chart the political and economic landscape that gave rise to HE in FE

To understand and uncover the daily 'lived experiences' of students who study HE in FE

To integrate and evaluate the findings from the above in order to explicate the characteristics of HE in FE and produce guidance for the sector

Research Questions (Chapter 1)

How did HE in FE develop and grow as a phenomenon and how did external intervention shape its essential nature?

How is the phenomenon then experienced by students who study HE in FE?

How do these experiences and interventions contribute to and intersect with the concept of HE-ness within an FE setting?

Literature review (Chapter 2)

Methodology (Chapter 3)

Autobiographical study (Chapter 4)

Deliberative policy analysis (Chapter 5)

Phenomenological study of HE in FE student experiences (Chapter 6)

Data collection and analysis

Historical policy analysis (Chapter 5)

Government data and statistics (Chapter 5)

Phenomenological case studies (Chapter 6)

Interviews

Personal writings/personal documents

Synthesis and contribution

Findings: An exposition of the nature and characteristics of HE in FE (Chapter 7)

Conclusions: FE in HE Management Principles (Chapter 8)

Figure 5.1   Diagrammatic representation of a doctoral study

candidate has shown how the aim, objectives and questions relate to each other and how these are followed through in terms of methodological approach and data collection. It also relates the material to its position within the thesis.

Possible Question Area: The contribution to knowledge made by the work

This may have been covered in the opening question, as discussed above. I would be surprised if you are not asked to explain this at some point in your viva.

Preparing your answer

Be very clear and positive about what you have achieved within your PhD study. What new knowledge have you created? Remember this doesn't need to be massive. Think about your final conclusions. How do they add to knowledge in your subject area? What do you expect the examiners to have learned from reading your thesis? A measure of your contribution can be gained by comparing your work to that of others. How does your work move the subject forward? What have you done that is different from the way that others have approached it? What gap in the literature does your work fill? Think about these aspects of your contribution, write them down, and prepare an answer which is short and to the point. The clearer you can make this, the more likely you are to convince the examiners that your work has made a contribution to knowledge and that you should be awarded a PhD. An example of how one student had framed her contribution was given in Figure 2.4 in Chapter 2 (p. 27).

Possible Question Area: Coverage of the literature and locating your own work within that context

The examiners will want to be sure that you understand the literature which underpins and surrounds your work. This is an important criterion for the award of PhD in that you are expected to show knowledge of the work of others that relates directly to your work and background studies which are important for your study. So it is likely that the examiners will ask some questions which test your knowledge of the academic literature within your subject. You may, for example, be asked: 'Which are the three most important papers which relate to your thesis?', 'Whose work has most influenced yours, and why?' or 'Whose work is the closest to yours?' and 'How is your work different from theirs?'

Preparing your answer

Don't worry about this. You will have read a lot of papers during the period of your PhD research. Your thesis will have a full list of references, or a bibliography, and you will have your thesis in front of you at the viva. In the days running up to your viva, re-read those papers which you feel are the most relevant to your own work. Think about those which are the most important and why. Have any papers emerged since you submitted your thesis? It is important that you continue to read the literature in your subject so that you remain up to date, and are able to quote recent, relevant papers. Produce a summary of the most important papers, as discussed in Chapter 4.

Possible Question Area: Methodological questions

The methodology, and the approach you have taken, is another area that the examiners are likely to want to discuss. This could come in the form of a question asking you to justify your approach: 'Why did you choose to use *Approach X*?' and 'What alternative approaches might you have chosen?' or more detailed questions about the methods used: 'Why did you use focus groups rather than interviews?' or 'How did you select the group of people to interview?'

Preparing your answer

Be clear in your own mind about the approach you have taken and why. Be prepared to refer to a paper or two, or a text, which sets out the approach you have taken. It is useful to be able to locate your methodological approach within other published work. Think about how your approach relates to your aim or question. What are the limitations of the approach that you have taken? Did you use the method fully, or did you choose aspects of it? If you have adapted a method, or used only elements of it, be clear about this.

Be very careful and clear in your use of terminology. I have seen many candidates use the terms 'methodology' and 'method' interchangeably, and they mean very different things in most subjects. If you have been studying in a practice-based subject and your practice is itself the methodology, be prepared to justify this. It might be useful to produce a checklist or table which shows how you considered the different methodologies available to you, and how you made your final choice of the methodology to use within your study. Figure 5.2 shows how one candidate compared three possible approaches within his thesis. (He ultimately chose to follow a case study approach, as presented by Yin (2009).) It is included here as an illustration of an approach which you might find helpful.

You will also need to be prepared to explain and discuss the stages of your work, how they were sequenced and the chronology of your study. Once again, scribbling down a diagram to represent this can be a useful way of reminding yourself of the sequence in which you did things during your study. Figure 5.3 shows how one student did this.

Methodology	Description	Alignment to my study	Reflections: Advantages/Disadvantages
Action research	Action research is a highly iterative and collaborative process. It involves cycles of planning, acting and evaluating change to a system. It is used to develop practical change and knowledge. Action research is underpinned by reflection throughout the entire research process.	Action research is well aligned with my project motivation to produce a practical, meaningful integrated and useful system which can have a substantial positive impact on my community of practice, and on the system users.	*Advantages*: underpinned by reflection as part of the process. It appears to be easy to understand and apply. It is collaborative and involves others, which is how I like to work. *Disadvantages*: Is this approach achievable within my proposed timeline? Action research implies a number of cycles, which may take significant time.
Soft systems	A process of seven stages: starting with establishing understanding, progressing through conceptualization to identifying changes and culminating with taking action. The approach allows the user to take multiple views of a system and the use of rich pictures provides a pictorial means of representing the system.	The collaborative nature of soft systems is aligned with the nature of my project. The staged nature could fit with the practical way in which my system is being developed.	*Advantages*: Systems thinking is, by design, built into the process, enabling an overall view to be taken. The rich picture will provide a useful means of conveying the system to others. *Disadvantages*: The staged approach may not completely fit with the stages which I am required to follow as part of the practical implementation of my system.
Case study	A very practical and questioning process which focuses on understanding the dynamics of an organisation using multiple views and different types of data collection to build detailed understanding of a particular situation context.	As I am working primarily within a single organisational setting, this could fit well with my study. The flexibility of multiple data collection and different views of the case appears a very good fit for the development of my system.	*Advantages*: Allows me to focus on a single organisation in detail. Appears it will be easier to manage and deliver within the context of my study site. *Disadvantages*: Does it provide the rigour that I need? I am not familiar with the method and will need to learn how to use it. Focusing on a single organisation will have limitations.

Figure 5.2 Comparing different methodological approaches

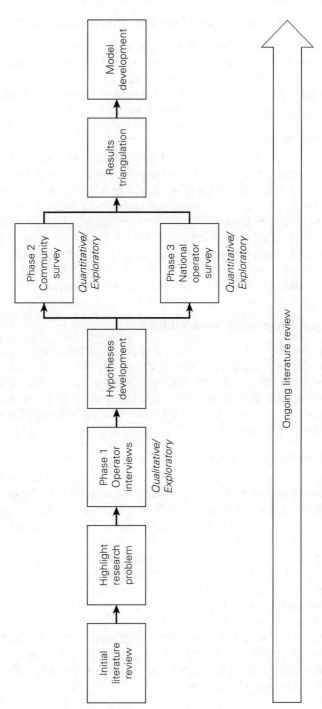

Figure 5.3 A timeline showing stages within a PhD study

Possible Question Area: Broader aspects of the work

You are expected to think about the broader aspects of your work, and could be asked about these in your viva. There is a push in many countries to look for the 'impact' of a research project, and to ensure that each piece of research has a clear purpose and produces something which is of use, in terms of economic, social or health benefits.

Preparing your answer

Think about the implications of your work. How might it be used or re-interpreted by others? Are there applications in other fields? What are the practical implications? Can your results be used in practice? Could they lead to a product of any sort? Have you addressed a problem which others may have considered, and if so, how can they use your findings within their own context? Could your study be 'scaled up' to provide a more general solution? And if so, how might this be done? What is the 'impact' of *your* work? Is there potential for economic, social or health benefits? Who would be interested in your work? Who could use it? Think about these issues.

Possible Question Area: Ethics

This will depend upon the subject of your PhD but, in my experience, there are always some ethical aspects to be taken into consideration. This may take the form of a specific question such as: 'Explain the ethical protocols and approval procedures which you followed' or 'Did you obtain informed consent?', or a more general question, such as: 'What are the ethical implications of this work?'

Preparing your answer

Think through the ethical issues that you have faced during your studies. How did your work impact on others, and how did you take account of that? Did you gain ethical approval from the university ethics committee? Did you inform your subjects as to the reason for your study, and of their rights within the study? In my experience, PhD candidates often underestimate the importance of ethics. It is something that some examiners take very seriously indeed, and you should be prepared for this. The level of importance will depend upon your subject area. In a laboratory study, or in a social science study, it is likely that the ethical protocols will have been made very clear to you by your supervisor and your university. In some subjects it may be less obvious. If necessary, discuss this aspect with your supervisor before your viva. I have seen a number of candidates who have been required to add a section on ethics to their thesis, because the examiners felt that they had not adequately addressed this.

Possible Question Area: The approach taken and the decisions made

Along the way, during your studies, you will have had to take several decisions as to the next step to take. The examiners may ask you to discuss and justify these. This could take the form of a very general question: 'What was the most important decision that you had to make during the course of your PhD?' or 'Which decisions would you change if you were to do the work again?' (Don't worry if you are asked something which mentions 'if you were to do it again'. In my experience this very, very rarely means that the examiners are going to ask you to change your decision or recommend more work.) Alternatively, the question might be much more specific: 'Why did you choose to test your system on this group of people?'

Preparing your answer

Think about the decisions that you made during your PhD studies. Write them down, if possible drawing a rough flowchart of how your work progressed over the whole period of your research. Think about any choices that you had to make. How did you make these? Were they the best choices? If not, why? Don't be frightened to admit that some of the choices that you made may not have been the best. It is important to show that you have learned from the PhD process.

Possible Question Area: Evaluation of your work

This area of questioning may take different forms depending upon the nature of your work. However, it is always important to show that you have, in some way, evaluated the work that you have done. This area is often overlooked, or underplayed, by candidates in the rush to get the work finished and the thesis written. Typical questions could be: 'How did you set about evaluating the work you did?', 'How does your work compare to that of others?', 'What is the strongest point of your work?', 'Which part of your thesis are you most proud of, and why?', and 'Which is the weakest part of your work?'

Preparing your answer

Think about how you compared your work with that of others. How successful has your study been? Did it achieve what you set out to do? If not, why? Go back to your original aim or question and look at it now. Did you fully achieve this? How do you know that you did? Don't be frightened to be honest here. The examiners are testing you to see if you can be critical about your own work, and that you are able to be objective about what you have, and have not, achieved.

Possible Question Area: Future work

Examiners will almost always ask about possible areas for future work. Questions could be: 'If you had another year, what would you do?' or 'How would you continue with the work? What are the next steps?' Don't worry if you are asked a question like this. It doesn't mean that the examiners are going to ask you to do another year's work!

Preparing your answer

You will already have some ideas for future possible directions for your work. Spend a little time thinking these through. What would be the next logical step? Which parts of the work could be published? If you have not already published your work in a journal, spend some time thinking about which aspects are publishable, and where they might be published. Part of your answer to a question like this could be a plan to publish some of the work in the future.

Possible Question Area: How studying for a doctorate has changed *you*

Remember that the examiners are assessing you, and whether you have reached doctoral standard. They may ask questions which relate directly to how the doctoral study process has impacted upon you as an individual and a researcher: 'What have you learned from doing this PhD?', 'How have you changed as a result of your studies?' or 'What advice would you give to a new PhD student who is just starting out on a similar topic to yours?' Questions like this are particularly common for candidates who have studied on a practice-based, or professional, doctorate because such programmes often place significant emphasis on personal transformation.

Preparing your answer

Think about what you have learned during your studies. You will, of course, have learned a lot about your subject area, but you will also have learned how to undertake research and how to apply certain methods. Think about how you have changed as a person since you started your PhD. It is likely that you are more reflective, more analytic in your approach and more critical. Be honest and authentic in your answer and you won't go far wrong. There are specific techniques for reflection, such as those of Schon (1983) presented in *The Reflective Practitioner: How Professionals Think in Action*.

Possible Question Area: Can you demonstrate critical thinking?

This will come through other questions, and isn't something that you will be asked directly. Questions in this category will refer to specifics within your thesis and could be: 'What evidence do you have for and against this?', 'How reliable is the evidence?' and 'What are the limitations of this part of the study?' The examiners will be looking for evidence of how you have synthesised and integrated different pieces of evidence, and how you have evaluated your own work and the work of others.

Preparing your answer

Always be prepared to question what you read, and your own work. The examiners are looking for deep, insightful understanding. Attending a mock viva and presenting your work to others will help in developing criticality. When you are re-reading your thesis try to constantly question what you read. You will almost certainly come across statements within your thesis which you may no longer fully agree with; that's good as it demonstrates that your arguments and research positions are continuing to develop. The important thing is to show that you have an open, questioning mind, and that you are able to grasp, question and integrate concepts to form new knowledge.

Possible Question Area: Independence

One of the fundamental purposes of the viva is to authenticate the work as your own. However, the viva also serves the purpose of testing your independence as a researcher. Are you capable of making your own decisions, or did you rely on your supervisor for all the major choices during your PhD studies? To award a doctorate the examiners need to be sure that you have the skills to undertake research of, and on, your own in the future. Questions in this category might include: 'What was the most important decision you made during your PhD?', 'How, and why, did you take that decision?' and 'If you were doing your PhD now, which things would you do differently?'

Preparing your answer

Think about the choices that you made during your research. When you are re-reading your thesis, make a note of the points at which you made important decisions. Think about how you made that decision. What evidence did you use? Why did you decide to proceed in the way that you did? Is there anything that, in hindsight, you would change or do differently?

One simple thing you can do is get used to saying 'I did this'. I have seen so many students refer to their work as 'We did this' during their viva. This gives the examiners the idea that some of the work may have been done by the student's supervisor or other members of a team (and sometimes that team is actually non-existent). Be clear; this is *your* PhD, and *you* did the work.

Possible Question Area: Why is the work worth a PhD?

A question like this may come at the start of the viva, as part of an opening question where you are asked to explain what you did and what the contribution is. Alternatively, it may be asked directly at any point during your viva, or as one of the last questions.

Preparing your answer

You will already have practised writing down and presenting your contribution to knowledge. You must highlight your contribution as an answer to any question asking why your work is worth the award of a PhD.

Possible Question Area: Have you any questions for us?

The examiners will normally finish by asking you if you have any final questions for them or 'anything that you wish to add in defence of your thesis' (or something like that).

Preparing your answer

You don't have to prepare an answer for either of these questions. In most of the vivas I have attended the candidate is quite tired by the end, and simply wants to get out of the room! So don't feel that you have to say anything. A simple 'No, thank you for reading my thesis and for giving me the opportunity to discuss my work with you' is fine. If, of course, there is something that you feel you should mention such as: 'Oh, I should have mentioned, I have just heard that my paper to the *International Journal of Tourism Studies* has been accepted for publication and will appear in the October issue', then do so.

The Abstract

The abstract is worth mentioning here because it has a special importance within the assessment process. Many universities ask a specific question of the examiners about the abstract. This is usually something like: 'Is the abstract presented satisfactory?'

Your abstract serves a particular purpose. It is the first thing that any potential reader will see and, based on the abstract, they will take a decision as to whether to read the thesis. The abstract should, on a single page, say what you have done, why you did it, how it relates to the work of others, and the contribution that your work makes. A sample abstract, taken from a PhD thesis of one of my students, is shown in Figure 5.4.

*   *   *

It is, of course, not possible to predict detailed questions relating to the specifics of your work. Each examiner will come to a viva with their own questioning style, and there will be very specific questions which relate directly

Abstract

In many developing countries telecentres have been set up in order to bring digital access to as many people as possible. There are issues with the sustainability of these centres from multiple perspectives; financial, social and cultural, political, technical and programmatic issues, any one of which could make a centre unsustainable. The majority of the existing literature has focused on India, Africa and South America with very few studies situated in the Philippines. This research addresses both the lack of empirical studies of factors that influence the sustainability of telecentres in the Philippines and in particular their use by individuals from rural communities. This research adopts a community-centred approach by focusing on the views and perceptions of users and non-users from the local community, to develop a model to guide community based telecentre initiatives. A wide range of issues were considered which had the potential to encourage or inhibit individual use of telecentres; these issues or themes were used to develop a new model.

Note: The candidate has stated the need for the work

The study consisted of three major phases; (1) a qualitative exploratory semi-structured interview administered to a sample of 13 telecentre operators, (2) a quantitative explanatory survey administered at 11 municipalities, and (3) utilisation of a data source from the National Computer Centre in the Philippines, consisting of a quantitative explanatory survey administered at the national level to all 257 telecentre operators. The research employed a mixed methods approach examining the views from the telecentre operators and the extensive fieldwork with rural communities. The qualitative and quantitative data were used to identify gaps in the expectations between the two main stakeholder groups and to elicit factors that contribute towards success and failure of telecentre-individual engagement. The qualitative study used thematic content analysis to analyse interview data, and identify common themes. The quantitative component of the study combined descriptive statistical tests to uncover patterns in the data and the use of chi square tests to identify associations between data.

Note: The candidate has stated what they did, and what methods they used

The critical success factors identified have been used to adapt existing models of telecentre sustainability to include a bottom up perspective from rural community stakeholders. The main contribution is the new model and the identification of a number of issues which encourage or inhibit individual use of a telecentre and thus influence the sustainability of telecentre projects. These issues include the physical characteristics of the centre, the operational and management approach, service availability, the nature and impact of local competition, and participation of stakeholder and community groups; all of which are moderated by individual community member demographics.

Note: The candidate has stated the outcome of the work, and the contribution which it makes

Figure 5.4   An example of an abstract from a PhD thesis

to your own thesis. This will probably involve the examiners asking you to go directly to a specific page and paragraph within your thesis, and to explain how and why you did something in that particular way. Don't be concerned about this. It is your thesis and you have spent three years or more doing the work, so you will understand the detail of what you have done.

However, if you cover the areas above before your viva, you will have addressed some of the questions that you are likely to face on the day. I have attempted to produce a list of questions that I could have been asked in my own viva, and these are included in Figure 5.5, as an example.

It is important to be confident about the work you have done (Day, 2009), and to show this in your answers. The examiners want to be able to pass you. They are looking for evidence that you fully understand the work, and that you can talk about it in a sensible and academic manner. You should prepare yourself as much as you can for the questioning on the day, but more than anything, you should be proud and positive about everything that you have achieved.

5.3 The questioning process

The section covers the nature of the questioning process, how to handle tricky and difficult questions, and how to interact with the examiners. The concept of 'defending' the work will be discussed. Tips will be given on what to do if you don't understand a question, or can't answer it.

> "Uncharacteristically, I felt very nervous, but my supervisor said that the panel could not detect it; she only knew because she could see my hands shaking under the table! I think the reason that I was so nervous was the thought of failure; all that work that had been done over a number of years and the thought of the panel not thinking it was worthy added to my anxiety. The dread I had was that I would be asked questions that I couldn't answer. In hindsight, I don't know why I inflicted this on myself. I thoroughly enjoyed the 'discussion' and felt very confident during the process because this was my work that I felt very passionate about and the time flew past! I was particularly pleased that all the examiners had said that they had enjoyed reading through my work and the discussion we had during the viva."

You know your work inside out; you should be positive and enthusiastic about it, and this should show during your viva. Be honest, authentic and passionate about your work; your examiners want to see and feel that you really *care* about what you have achieved. Answer politely and never lose your temper even if you don't agree with what an examiner is saying. Try to relax and enjoy the discussion and answer confidently.

Some questions that I might have been asked in my own PhD viva

Note, my own PhD viva was a long time ago (some 35 years ago as I write this) and I can't remember any of the questions I was asked. My subject was mathematics and I had produced a mathematical model which predicted heat flow within a human when subjected to various different conditions and climates.

- Tell us, in 5 to 10 minutes, about your work, highlighting what you did, why you did it, and what the contribution is.

- You have built a mathematical model which predicts heat flow within a human subject. Why? What is the purpose of your study? And whose idea was it?

- Explain your main research question. Your study included a series of experiments. What were the hypotheses for each of those experiments?

- Which are the most important papers which relate to your own work?
- Whose model has most influenced yours, and why?
- You chose to use the finite element method for the basis of your model. Why did you choose to use the finite element method over an alternative, such as the finite difference method?
- Are there any other approaches which you might have taken?

- You developed your own computer programs to test the models. Explain to us the process you used to design and test your programs.

- Where did you get the data to test your models? How realistic are the data?
- How do you results compare to the real world? And to the models of others?

- Who will use the work? How much more work would be needed to convert your computer program into something which could be marketed? Could the model that you have produced be used within any other application areas?

- Were there any ethical issues which came up during your studies?
- What was the most important decision that you had to make?
- Are there any decisions which you would change if you were to do the work again?
- How could your models be improved?

- What is the strongest point of your work, and the best thing about your models?
- Which is the weakest part of your work? And what are the limitations of your models?

- If you had another year, what would you do next? How could your models be improved?

- What have you learned from doing this PhD? Specifically what have you learned about numerical modelling and about mathematical modelling in general? What advice would you give to others who might be considering using the finite element method as a basis for development of their own models?

Figure 5.5   Some sample questions, based on my own PhD thesis

Listen carefully to each question. If you don't understand a question, it is quite acceptable to ask the examiner to repeat it. If you need time to think before your answer; that is also fine. It is an examination, so your answers are important, and the questions will need your careful and focused consideration.

If you don't agree with something an examiner in saying, that is also acceptable, but you will need to give a logical and considered reason, supported by evidence from your thesis (and/or the literature). If an examiner raises a point and you realise that something you have said in the thesis may not be quite correct, or a position that you have taken is perhaps not as well-founded as you had thought when you wrote it, it is better to agree, and admit you are wrong. I have seen several students who start to argue with the examiner when it is obvious that they are on shaky ground. I guess they felt that admitting that something is not quite right was a weakness. On the contrary, one of the fundamentals of academic debate is considering the views of peers and accepting, reviewing and reacting to academic criticism.

It is easy to take any criticism very personally. I could say that the criticism is about the work, rather than you. But of course you feel so close to the work, and you have such an emotional attachment to it, that the natural reaction is to take it personally. You need to be aware of this, and react to any criticisms which arise during your viva in a calm, reasoned, measured and logical way. Also, remember that it is acceptable to admit to any mistakes that you made during the course of your PhD studies. Indeed, it is to be encouraged. It is important to show how you learned from your mistakes.

"Don't 'take on' the examiners. There are ways of conveying that you have a different view point to the examiners. Engage in discussion with them, but don't argue with them."

The phrase 'defence of your thesis' is often used in the context of the PhD viva. I sometimes think it is an ill-chosen use of the word 'defence' because it has unpleasant and confrontational connotations. In terms of the viva, the word 'defence' refers to defending your work through the use of evidence and logical argument, and being able to put together such arguments in the answers to questions.

5.4 What examiners are looking for and how they prepare their questions

When I receive a thesis for examination the first thing I will do is skim through it, stopping at the abstract, the introduction and the conclusions. I will read through those sections first to get a 'feel' for what the thesis is about, what the candidate set out to achieve, and what the contribution is. I should be able to glean an overview of those areas from a first read through those parts of the thesis. I also look at the reference list to get a feel for the work that the candidate has read, to check for recent references, and to see if they have published any papers themselves. I will then put the thesis down, and return to it over the next few weeks as I approach the examination, reading through it sequentially and thoroughly.

I have a bank of standard questions which I will always ask a candidate, similar to those which I have already covered within this chapter. I will modify these standard questions to make them specific to the thesis I am examining. I will also start to compile a list of questions which are very specific to the thesis. Personally I like to write them directly on my copy of the thesis. In this way, if a question relates directly to a specific issue within the thesis, I will be on the correct page as I ask the question. Many examiners I have worked with produce a typed list of questions. I will mark the position of each question in the thesis with a sticky note, as shown in Figure 5.6.

Most examiners I have worked with mark up a thesis in a similar manner. Don't be frightened when your examiners turn up with theses decorated with a lot of sticky notes. This doesn't mean that the examiners have lots of problems with your work. It simply shows that they have prepared well, have read your thesis thoroughly, and that they are treating the event with the seriousness, and respect, that it deserves (that is, that they are doing their job properly!).

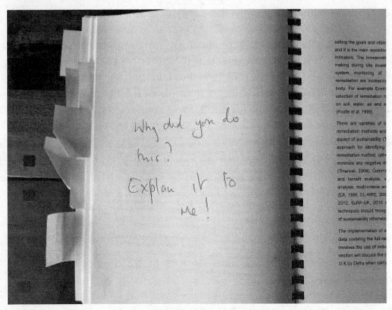

Figure 5.6   A thesis marked up with sticky notes

Note: I usually write my questions on the thesis, on the page opposite the relevant text, and mark the position with a sticky note.

Professor Simon Leather, says on his blog entry 'Are PhD examiners really ogres?' (2013):

> *"I don't see a PhD viva as a gladiatorial contest; rather a friendly, but search-ing discussion of the methods used, a critical discussion of the analysis of the results obtained and an opportunity to understand how and why they interpreted the results as they did. I always begin by telling the candidate how much I enjoyed reading their thesis and tell them not to worry unduly about the Sticky notes festooning the sides of my copy of their thesis, most are usually typos and many are in the references section where students seem to become incredibly careless. As I tell them; if you can't be bothered to format your references properly, what message am I to take home about your experimental procedures?"*

I agree with Professor Leather. I must have read more than 100 PhD theses, and so many of them suffered from problems with referencing. The major-ity of these were simple errors which, with a little more care and attention, would have been sorted out before submission. The most common referenc-ing problems include: papers which are cited in the text but don't appear in the reference list, papers which appear in the reference list but aren't cited within the text, and simply not following a standard referencing style such as Harvard (or following it to some extent, but not precisely and consistently). In some subject areas it is standard practice to use footnotes, as well as refer-ences. The same principles apply; these footnotes should be used correctly.

In some cases, I also find a lot of typographical and grammatical errors. This shouldn't happen, and is incredibly frustrating for the examiner. If I do find typos I will try to mark these up on the thesis, so that I can give my marked copy to the candidate after the viva, and they can then use it in preparing the final version. If there are lots of errors throughout the thesis, I will probably get so frustrated that I will only mark the first couple of chapters, and leave the candidate and their supervisor to sort out the rest after the viva.

Quoting Professor Leather again:

> *"I always ask the candidate what they did before and why they ended up doing the PhD that I am examining. I try to make the discussion a mixture of general wider-reaching issues and consideration of the material in each chapter. At all times, even if I feel that there is a fault, I approach the matter in a supportive and advisory role. This is characteristic of **all** the external and internal examiners that I have observed over the years."*

Again, I agree. Examiners are generally looking for the positives in your work, and if they do spot a problem, they are thinking about how it might be explained or corrected. They will understand that you have spent three or more years studying for your PhD, and will respect that. After all, they will have PhD students of their own (and will once have been one themselves; albeit possibly many years ago).

I will aim to have a few questions for each and every chapter. As I get further engrossed in reading the thesis, I will become genuinely interested in what they did, why they did it, and how they chose to approach it. I will be looking to learn something from what they have done, and from the viva process.

Figures 5.7, 5.8 and 5.9 include some example questions based on the preliminary reports of examiners. These have been drawn from a number of reports, but have been rewritten to ensure anonymity and for ethical reasons. They represent the type of questions that examiners form when reading a thesis in preparation for a viva, and are adapted from examiners' reports in three disciplines: art and design, business and management, and social science. You will see that some of the questions are quite general (particularly those in Figure 5.7) while others are very specific to the thesis, referring to particular sections, figures and tables (see Figures 5.8 and 5.9).

This PhD thesis presents a critical reflection on an important and highly relevant body of work that has been created and exhibited within the public domain over a period of more than a decade. Much has happened and developed in this area of practice during this time. The candidate has played a significant role in the progression and development of this creative medium, and is to be applauded for the contribution which has been made to contemporary practice. The resulting work, experimentation and evaluation provide a strong starting point for many emerging artists in the future. The submitted thesis provides a detailed contextual backdrop against which the researcher's creative practice is discussed and illuminated. Overall, therefore, there is much to recommend in this submission, both in the practical aspects of the work and the artefacts produced, and in the way the thesis underpins these with theory and explores the conceptual contribution of the work.

During the viva I would wish to discuss the following with the candidate:

- What is the primary strength of this submission? Is it the visual, aesthetic, theoretical, technical or a synthesis of all of these?
- What is original? Where does the novelty lie? Is it in the practical or the conceptual or both? How would the candidate define the contribution to knowledge? And the contribution to practice? Are the two intertwined?
- Why has the candidate selected the examples presented? How did the methodology for inclusion develop? This is not about the method for each individual exemplar but about the totality of the evaluation.
- What are the strongest and weakest parts of the submission, and why?
- How would the candidate describe the creative/technical achievements?
- What has been the overall impact of the work? How have others benefitted from the candidate's practice?
- Are there examples of critical evaluations of the projects in the public domain?
- How will the candidate's practice develop in the future?

Figure 5.7 Preliminary questions of an examiner for a practice-based PhD in art and design

Note. In this case the PhD thesis presented and discussed a significant body of art work which had been exhibited and thus presented within the public domain.

Chapter 1

Explain the motivation and the aim of the work. How were the research questions formulated? What was the history behind the study?

Chapter 2

Did the candidate seek to systematically explore why the efforts of the national body failed?

What evidence was there that policy and computer systems were real barriers to implementation?

How does the candidate's own professional background, described in Chapter 2, contribute specifically to the contribution and to the formulation of the research questions?

Chapter 3

What exactly are 'internal services', and how can this concept lead to a wider application of them? (page 29)

Barriers – did the candidate explore the initial set-up costs? Work cultures? Did she explore the literature on cultural issues related to acquisitions and mergers? (page 42)

What about strategy? (page 44)

What were the things that made the published case studies so successful? (page 46)

Chapter 4

I would like a verbal explanation of how Tables 4.4 & 4.5 were derived and relate this to the material covered in the previous chapters.

I would like a verbal explanation of how the ticks have been assigned to the boxes in Table 4.6.

Chapter 5

How were the interviews conducted? (page 75) How were participants selected? What ethical approvals were sought and gained?

Why were some projects not covered, and some people not selected? (page 77)

How were the themes arrived at? Were some of the themes a foregone conclusion, particularly given the design of the interview questions? (page 81)

Did the candidate consider how the key barriers had been overcome in the case studies? (page 93) Which ones had not been overcome?

Fig 5.3: I would like to interrogate this with the candidate. What is the significance of column 3? What contribution did the case study make to the overall contribution to knowledge?

Chapter 6

How will the work be developed in the future? Are the users committed to carrying it forward?

Figure 5.8   Preliminary questions of an examiner for a PhD in business and management

This is an interesting and engaging thesis which I enjoyed reading. It raises a number of pertinent questions, and explores some interesting, and potentially important, aspects of social care. There are some areas which I would like to explore further with the candidate during the viva. These are largely for the purposes of clarification; there are certain areas of the work which need further explanation and warrant discussion during the viva. I will outline these areas below.

The first point is the philosophical underpinnings of the thesis. The work is housed in praxis, and draws upon the theories of several important scholars. Fuller exploration of the philosophical underpinning of the work is required. Some of the theoretical underpinnings are articulated well; the work of Bourdieu and Foucault is mentioned early in the thesis, but this is not developed further in the rest of the thesis. I would like to explore how their work influenced the thesis, and the methodological approach taken. What is exactly meant by 'social capital' in the context of this study (page 76)?

I was interested in the discussion of the different models of inclusion. I would wish to discuss how these specific models were derived and how they relate to published models from the literature.

The construction of the sample was clearly explained but I have some issues relating to location – why not look at one geographical area in depth, rather than sampling across several areas? Is the candidate convinced that the sample chosen enabled sufficient depth of analysis?

I was a little unclear about the process of data analysis. Was a software package used? How were the themes derived? I would like to discuss this during the viva, and I would like the candidate to take me through the analysis process in some detail.

Did the researcher consider getting peers to interview the subjects, rather than personally undertake the interviews?

I got the impression that the subjects were treated as a homogeneous group; and they are not. Gender, class and race (e.g. page 102) are important issues. Were these considered in any detail, and if not, why? The issue of social exclusion also warrants discussion in the viva (particularly in relation to Chapter 4).

The conclusions drawn are sensible, useful, and in keeping with the thrust of the research. The contribution made by the work could be put more strongly in Chapter 7.

There are some typographical errors, and some issues of formatting (particularly with respect to the figures in Chapters 5 and 6). There is also a slight overreliance on quotes. I spotted some errors of referencing which will need correcting in the final thesis.

Overall, I found this an interesting thesis, which I enjoyed reading. I feel confident that there is a contribution to knowledge within this work.

I look forward to discussing it in more depth with the candidate during the oral examination.

Figure 5.9   Preliminary questions of an examiner for a PhD in social science

5.5 Exercises

▶ Produce your own list of typical questions, based on the list of question areas given below. Remember that the list here contains questions of a general nature and that it is not possible to predict the questions what will arise from the examiners reading your thesis.

Possible Question Area
The 'Opening' Question.
The Abstract
The motivation for, and purpose of, the work.
The aim / objectives / research question / hypotheses.
The contribution to knowledge made by the work.
Coverage of the literature and locating your own work within that context.
Methodological questions.
Broader aspects of the work.
Ethics.
The approach taken and the decisions made.
Evaluation of your work.
Future work.
How studying for a doctorate has changed you.
Why is the work worth a PhD?
Have you any questions for us?

Summary

This chapter has covered some typical questions that might come up during your viva and how you might approach answering them. The next chapter includes a simulation of an entire viva, to give you an idea of how the viva process can play out on the day.

6 The Viva Itself

On completion of this chapter you will:

▶ understand the nature of the viva process
▶ have a deeper understanding of how the viva process operates and something of what could happen during a viva
▶ feel more confident about your own viva
▶ be better prepared for your own viva, and continue with your preparations

6.1 Chapter overview

This chapter plays out an entire viva. The account is fictional, but draws from aspects of real student PhD examinations which I have attended. First, I simulate the preliminary stages of the viva, including the examiners' private pre-meeting, highlighting the role of the preliminary reports. I then go on to simulate some possible situations that might arise during the viva and show how the candidate reacts to these. Finally, I will cover the post-viva private meeting of the examiners while they deliberate the outcome, and how that outcome is relayed to the candidate. I also include some mock documentation to illustrate the type of forms which the examiners are likely to complete for the university.

I will include discussion on the length of the viva, which can vary substantially from the view that 'three hours is what the candidate deserves after all their work' (that is, one hour for each year of candidature) through to '80–90 minutes is respectful and any longer is a waste of everyone's time'.

Health Warning

I did wonder whether or not it was appropriate to include this chapter. I realise that it is impossible to produce a 'model' of a viva because each one is so different and so specific to the candidate's thesis. In a similar way to the mock viva, it is not possible to predict the questions that you will encounter in your own viva, and you must remember that when you read this chapter. In the end, however, I decided that I should include it to illustrate the viva process, and give you an example of how a viva can play out. Please use it to gain an understanding of the entire viva process, but don't expect that your own viva will be the same, or that the questions will be similar. The questions that I have included here are, by necessity, generalised in order to illustrate the flow and sequence of the viva process, so please treat them as such. Having finished my health warning, I do hope that you will find the chapter useful, and that it will help to 'de-mystify' the viva process a little.

6.2 Preamble

Jonathan has undertaken a PhD in Archaeology. He has recently submitted his thesis and his examination is taking place today. Jonathan has done a lot of work, and his supervisor has been telling him that he 'should be OK', but he is still very nervous about his viva. He felt that he was a bit rushed towards the end of his studies, and realises that the final stages of his work, and his thesis write-up suffered a little as a result.

The examination team for his thesis is:

- Professor Derek Koyne (external examiner)
- Dr Susan West (internal examiner)
- Professor Keith Turns (independent Chair)

Jonathan will be accompanied in the examination by his supervisor, Dr Forest. Jonathan had a lazy, relaxing evening the night before his viva, and was up early in the morning to make sure that he arrived at the viva room in plenty of time. He has arranged to meet Dr Forest at his office at 9.30am. They have been informed that the viva is likely to start some time around 10am, and that someone will come to Dr Forest's office and collect them.

6.3 The pre-meeting

The time is 9.30 am.

The examiners and the Chair meet for a pre-meeting to discuss their views on the thesis and to decide on the approach to be taken during the examination. Professor Koyne and Dr West have both completed their initial assessment forms, and submitted these to the university. Their comments, taken from the forms, can be seen in Figure 6.1 (Professor Koyne) and Figure 6.2 (Dr West).

Professor Koyne is one of the most eminent experts in the field of Jonathan's thesis. He is an experienced examiner, having previously examined more than 20 PhD candidates. Professor Koyne has methodological concerns with the work, and feels that the evaluation is inadequate.

Dr West thinks that the thesis is probably acceptable for PhD, subject to some corrections. She feels that the research questions, as presented, are a little too general and could be improved to more closely match the detail of what has been done. (Professor Koyne has also made a similar point in his preliminary report.) This is her first PhD oral examination, and she is quite nervous. She does not know Jonathan, but she is aware of his work, and once attended a departmental seminar where he was presenting.

Professor Turns, as Chair, arrives at the room first to check everything is in order, and places a notice on the door so that they won't be disturbed (Figure 6.3). He also checks that the coffee which he requested has arrived

UNIVERSITY OF NEVERLAND

Preliminary written comments on a research degree thesis

Name of Examiner: Professor Derek Koyne

Name of Candidate: Jonathan Foxton

Title of Thesis: An Investigation into Y

The subject of enquiry is interesting and topical. There is evidence that the candidate has worked extremely hard in gathering data for his study. The candidate has a thorough understanding of the subject, and has drawn evidence from a variety of published sources.

Chapter 1 provides the background to the work, the motivation for doing the study and introduces the research questions. The research questions seem quite general and I would wish to discuss these with the candidate during the viva voice examination. I feel that they could be reformulated in a more rigorous and precise manner.

Chapter 2. Literature review. The literature review is good, and shows evidence of critical thinking.

Chapter Three. Research Methodology. The candidate refers to several different approaches. However, these are presented in a quite descriptive manner, and is not clear to me exactly which approach has been taken. The candidate does not explain or justify the specific methodological approach which he has taken.

Chapters Four, Five and Six. These chapters contain the detail of the work. It is clear that the candidate has undertaken a substantial study, and has derived some interesting findings. However, I didn't see any explanation of how the data were analysed. A series of themes are presented with little discussion as to how these were derived.

Chapter Seven. Evaluation. I feel this is one of the weakest areas of the work. The candidate has largely given his own views on the study and the results with little reference to the literature. There are several other studies which are similar to his own (e.g. Strong, 2006, and Hui, 2010) and he could, and should, have compared his results to theirs.

Chapter Eight. Conclusion. This is good, with coverage of areas for future work. However, I felt he could have returned to his initial research questions in either this chapter or in the previous chapter and discussed how successful the study was in terms of those research questions.

General comments:

Overall, the subject of enquiry is important and the thesis makes a useful contribution to the subject.

I feel that the candidate has made a contribution to knowledge, however I have concerns with the thesis as it is currently presented. I would wish to discuss the issues above with the candidate during the viva, and wish to reserve judgement as to award of the degree until after the viva voice examination.

There are a number of typographical and grammatical errors and the thesis must be thoroughly checked and revised to remove these. Given the nature of the subject and the number of acronyms used, there is the need for a 'Glossary of Terms', perhaps to be placed after the Contents Page.

Figure 6.1   Professor Koyne's preliminary report

UNIVERSITY OF NEVERLAND

Preliminary written comments on a research degree thesis

Name of Examiner: Doctor Susan West
Name of Candidate: Jonathan Foxton
Title of Thesis: An Investigation into Y

This thesis is well-structured, and generally well-written. I did notice some grammatical and typographical errors which will need correction in the final version of the thesis. The work is supported by a significant list of references in Harvard format.

The background to the work, and the need for the model, is clearly justified in Chapter 1. A set of general questions are set out. I think these questions are perhaps a little broad, and would wish to discuss the logic behind their production with the candidate during the viva. I also note that the candidate does not explicitly return to the aims at the end of the thesis to discuss whether they have been achieved, although an evaluation is presented which does, in general, cover the same issues as expressed within the aims.

Chapter 2 presents a comprehensive review of the literature underpinning the study. I would like to discuss with the candidate how the literature informed the study, and how the methodological approach was chosen.

Chapter 3 presents the methodological approach. The candidate has chosen a particular combination of methods for the study. I would like to discuss with the candidate the justification for the choice of methods, and the construction of the case study. How representative and realistic is the case study? How were the elements of the study chosen and why?

Chapter 4, 5 and 6 present the collection and analysis of data, and the development of a model. The model is tested through the use of an illustrative case study, which illuminates the model in some significant detail. I would like to discuss the reliability of the results and the limitations of the study. How generalizable are the results? What are the opportunities for 'scale-up' to a more realistic scenario?

Chapter 7 presents some comparisons of the model with the work of others. It also discusses the implications of the work, and Chapter 8 draws conclusions, and identifies areas for future work. Although it is implicit within these discussions, the candidate does not explicitly state the contribution made by the work. I would like to ask the candidate to be more explicit about this in the viva discussion and to evaluate the work in terms of the published work of others. I would like to discuss who might use the work, how and why?

It is clear that the candidate has undertaken a significant study, applying appropriate research methods. The thesis demonstrates a grasp of the relevant literature. There is evidence of criticality. The study has produced some interesting results which have the potential to be of use. It seems to me that the work is of doctoral standard, and has resulted in a contribution to knowledge.

My initial recommendation would be that the candidate should Pass and be awarded the degree of PhD, subject to a satisfactory performance in the viva, and correction of relatively minor thesis issues.

I look forward to an interesting discussion with the candidate during the viva.

Figure 6.2   Dr West's preliminary report

Figure 6.3   The door of the examination room

(very important; and, luckily, yes it has arrived). Dr West arrives shortly afterwards. Neither of them has met Professor Koyne before, although they are aware of him by reputation.

Soon the phone rings; Professor Koyne has arrived at the reception desk downstairs. Professor Turns goes down to collect him, and brings him to the room. He does the introductions and pours the coffee. They all sit down to discuss Jonathan's work. Professor Turns has copies of both examiners' preliminary reports. He gives copies to both examiners and allows them a few minutes to read each other's report.

Professor Koyne starts: 'I think this candidate has done some good work and in general I do feel that he has just about reached the standard. But I am concerned that he hasn't fully explained his methodological approach, justified it, or said exactly how he did things and went about analysing the data. I also feel that the thesis tails off towards the end. I think he should have spent more time evaluating the work and comparing his results with those of others. So these are the areas that I would like to discuss with him during the viva. I also spotted a number of typos and I've marked them up on my copy of the thesis, which I can leave with him at the end of the viva.'

Dr West: 'I thought it was a good thesis. I too noticed some typographical errors and I've also marked up my copy. I hadn't picked up on the issues that you raised, Derek, but on reflection I agree with you. I also feel that the research questions could have been better formulated and I would like to explore that aspect of the thesis.'

Professor Turns: 'How would you like to organise the questioning? Should we go through the thesis chapter by chapter?'

Professor Koyne: 'I would suggest that we start by asking the candidate to explain what he has done, why he did it and why it is worth a PhD in, say, 5 to 10 minutes. We can then go through the thesis chapter by chapter. I have questions I would like to ask in almost every chapter of the thesis. When we come to the methodology chapter and the later chapters I will concentrate on the areas that I mentioned. Is that OK with you, Susan?'

Dr West: 'Yes that's fine. I also have some questions on most chapters so I am happy for us to move through the thesis on a chapter-by-chapter basis'.

Professor Turns: 'Good. That sounds like it will work. Professor Koyne; can I leave to you to start then please? I would suggest that we aim for the viva to last around a couple of hours. I'll keep my eye on my watch and let you know how time is progressing after the halfway mark. Is that OK?'

Professor Koyne and Dr West nod their heads to signify their agreement to the plan. They discuss where they will sit, and where Jonathan should sit. Professor Turns points out that Jonathan will be accompanied by his supervisor, Dr Forest. The examiners suggest that Dr Forest should sit a little away from Jonathan so that he can observe, but is not directly in the sightline of Jonathan (in case that distracts him). Professor Koyne pours a glass of water for Jonathan.

The time is now 10.05am. Professor Koyne leaves the room and goes to collect Jonathan and Dr Forest from Dr Forest's office.

6.4   The viva

The time is 10.10am. Jonathan and Dr Forest enter the room. Professor Turns introduces the candidate and his supervisor to the examiners. Jonathan is invited to sit opposite the examiners, and Dr Forest sits on the same side of the table as Jonathan, a little away from him. Professor Turns sits between the two examiners.

Jonathan is very nervous about his examination. He recognises that at the end he was quite rushed, and he didn't spend as much time evaluating his work as he would have liked. He found writing the thesis a very difficult exercise, and gave many drafts to Dr Forest. Nonetheless, he hopes that he has done enough and he is ready to defend his work.

Professor Turns: 'Welcome Jonathan. I'd like to explain the process this morning. My colleagues Professor Koyne and Dr West have read your thesis, and have enjoyed doing so. They each have some questions that they would like to ask you. We are aiming to keep the viva as friendly and informal as possible; however, it is a formal examination of you and your thesis. My colleagues will ask their questions, moving through your thesis chapter by chapter. We expect the viva to take around two hours. If you need to take a break at any time, or if there is anything that you need, just let us know. Professor Koyne will start the questions.

Professor Koyne: 'Hello Jonathan. I've enjoyed reading your work. Could we start by you giving us a short overview of what you have done, why you did it, and also why you think it is worth a PhD? Around 5 to 10 minutes please.'

Jonathan has prepared for this question and has rehearsed his answer with his supervisor. He starts: 'I graduated with my degree in Archaeology three years ago, and was fascinated by the subject so decided I wanted to continue to do a PhD and further research. I chose this topic because I found there was a gap in the literature; specifically Hui, Komass and others had done work in a similar area but their studies were specific to the subject of X, while I felt that there was a need for a study of Y. This is backed up by the work of Tubert who indicated that Y is a much under-researched and yet important area.'

Jonathan goes on to briefly explain the detail of his study, the data he collected and the main results. He then continues: 'I believe that my work is worth a PhD because it has made a contribution to the study of Y. The results I have obtained are novel and different from those produced by previous studies'.

You should by now have prepared your own answer to a question like this. Jonathan's statement is quite general. Your own answer should be much more specific, outlining the actual work that you have done.

Professor Koyne: 'Many thanks. We will now start to work through your thesis chapter by chapter. Let's start with the abstract. I felt that what you have just said was good. In fact, you expressed what you have done and the contribution that you have made much better than you did here in the abstract. I think you need to bring your contribution out much more strongly in the abstract of your thesis. The abstract is the first thing any reader will see when they open your thesis, and it will be on the basis of the abstract that they decide whether to read any further or not. So your abstract needs to be very clear as to what you did, how and why you did it, and what contribution it resulted in. Can you now please turn to page 3 in Chapter 1.'

Jonathan turns the pages of his copy of the thesis to page 3.

Professor Koyne: 'I would like to discuss your research questions. We both felt that they were perhaps a little too general. Could you explain how you derived them, please'.

Jonathan talks through his research questions, making some reference to the literature which he feels informed his questions. In doing so, he can see what Professor Koyne is driving at: 'Yes now that I have explained them

I realise that you are right. Questions 1 and 2 overlap and could be made more precise. These are the questions that I started with, but on reflection I perhaps should have revised them to more closely match the questions that I actually answered in the end.'

Dr West: 'I'm pleased that you said that Jonathan. There is nothing wrong with reviewing and revising your questions as you study proceeds. I suspect that we might ask you to revisit these and produce a more precise and updated version'.

The examiners continue working through the thesis, chapter by chapter. They try to phrase their questions carefully and be as supportive as possible. They are both quite happy with Chapter 2, which is Jonathan's literature review. They ask some points of clarification, and some further questions to test Jonathan's knowledge of the literature.

They then turn to Chapter 3, the methodology chapter, which Professor Koyne is concerned about.

Professor Koyne: 'Can you turn to Chapter 3, Jonathan and go to page 65. Can you talk through your methodological approach, and explain which methods you used.'

Jonathan considered several methods, and in the end decided to use a mixed methods approach. He realises now that he probably hasn't done himself justice in the thesis, and in his answer he tries to explain how he chose the particular methods, how he used them and the theoretical approach which underpins them. He feels that he gives a good answer, and can see that both Professor Koyne and Dr West are smiling and nodding their heads as he speaks, which reassures him.

Professor Koyne: 'Now, what you said there is much better than the way that you have written it in your thesis. I think that you need to explain it a bit better in the thesis and add some references to the literature to justify your use of mixed methods.'

Dr West:' Yes I agree.'

The examiners ask some specific questions about some of the detail within the methodology chapter, and then move to Chapter 4, which is the point in the thesis where Jonathan begins to present his study, the approach taken, the data collected and the results obtained. The examiners take turns in asking Jonathan to explain some of the details about the work.

The questioning focuses on a series of figures in Chapter 5. Dr West asks Jonathan to explain some of the details of the figures, which contain a set of graphs. The examiners' copies of the thesis are not in colour and she is finding it difficult to differentiate between the different curves in the graphs. Jonathan tries to explain.

Dr West: 'Can you take us through Figure 5.6 to 5.9 please. You will find them on pages 145 onwards. It might be easier if you use the whiteboard. There are some pens beside the board'.

Jonathan goes to the whiteboard and draws a quick diagram, talking through each curve, how it was derived from the data and what it signifies.

Dr West: 'I am beginning to understand now. I think you need to find a way to present these graphs in the thesis which is much more understandable to the reader. You must label each one clearly and it is probably better to use broken lines and a legend, rather than the way you have tried to use colour. Otherwise you are going to have to print each final copy of your thesis in full colour'.

Professor Koyne: 'In Figure 5.7 on page 157 the axes need labelling. And Figure 5.8 needs a title. Oh, and I don't think you refer to Figure 5.9 at all. I believe that figures should always be referred to somewhere in the text. After all, you must have thought it worth including the figure, so it must be worthy of discussion within the text. You'll need to correct these things in the final copy of your thesis.'

Jonathan sits down again, quite relieved that this part of the examination is over. He takes a drink of water.

Professor Turns looks at his copy of the thesis. The examiners are now on page 165, and the time is 11.20pm. There are 245 pages in the thesis, so the examiners are more than half way through their work. They are running just about to time. However, Professor Turns gently reminds them of the time.

The examiners continue to work through the thesis chapter by chapter, stopping when one of them has a question. They reach Chapter 7, which is entitled 'Evaluation'.

Professor Koyne starts: 'I think we are now finished with Chapter 6. Can you please turn to page 172, which is where Chapter 7 begins. Now you have called this Chapter 7 'Evaluation' but I don't think it is. Can you explain please?'

Jonathan is a little confused now. As far as he is concerned this chapter presents an evaluation of the work. After all, he has discussed the work here, and in some detail, so he doesn't understand what Professor Koyne is getting at: 'I'm sorry. I didn't understand the question. Would you mind asking it again please?'

Professor Koyne: 'Yes, of course. What I expect of an evaluation is a detailed discussion of your results, their implications, and for you to return to the literature and compare your results to those of others. Now I see some of the former; that is, you have discussed your results and said something about the possible implications. But I don't think you have considered how your work compares with the work of other researchers who are working in your field. There are several other studies which are similar to yours, for example, those of Strong – I think it was published in her paper of 2006 – and Hui et al. – I think they published their latest paper in 2010. Are you aware of their work? And did you compare your results to theirs?'

Jonathan: 'Oh, sorry, I see what you mean now. Yes, I read the work of Strong and I did do some comparisons of her results against mine. I have the results of that comparison in my note book. I didn't think of including it here. Would you like me to get my note book?'

Professor Koyne: 'No there's no need to get your note book. Can you tell us now what the comparison showed please?'

Jonathan: 'Can I just have a minute to think please?'

Professor Koyne: 'Yes of course'.

Jonathan spends a few moments quietly thinking and reminding himself of that piece of work. It is over a year since he did it, but he can just about remember the main points. He starts to speak again: 'Yes I remember. In general my model showed a closer approximation to the real situation, particularly using the data from my case study. In particular I was much closer with respect to factors 7 and 9. And factor 9, as we discussed earlier, is one of the three most important factors'.

Professor Koyne:' That sounds good, and worth including in the thesis. Would you be able to include a table showing these results in Chapter 7?'

Jonathan: 'Yes, I still have the details in my note book, so I could do that'.

Professor Koyne: 'And the work of Hui et al.?'

Jonathan: 'I've seen an early paper of Hui's, and I know the types of model that his group has been trying to develop, but I haven't seen their latest paper, which must be the one which you are talking about. All of the earlier work that I have seen did not include any details of the model in terms of the parameters that it is based on, so I couldn't really make a comparison. But I understand the difference between my model and theirs.'

Professor Koyne: 'I've seen a more recent paper. I'll send you a copy and you should have a look and see if you can find a way of comparing your work with theirs'.

The examiners continue their questioning and move to Chapter 8. They also spend a little time on the reference list; Dr West points out some errors in the referencing style.

Dr West: 'I have a final question. Did you consider publishing any of the work?'

Jonathan: 'Yes. I'd been focusing on getting my thesis finished, but since I've submitted I've been discussing publishing some of the work with Dr Forest. We have identified a journal that we think is suitable and I've produced a first draft of a paper'.

Dr West: 'That's good. Good luck with the paper. I think it is important that this work gets published. There are some interesting results here and I think it would be a shame if you didn't publish at least one paper. That's my final question; thank you'. Dr West turns to Professor Turns to signify that she has finished her questions.

Professor Turns asks both examiners if they have finished their questioning. They nod to indicate that they have. The viva has lasted approximately two hours, which is probably around average.

Professor Turns: 'Jonathan; my colleagues have completed their questioning which brings us to the end of your viva. We will shortly ask you and your supervisor to withdraw so that we can discuss the outcome. But before we do so, is there anything that you would like to say, anything that you would like to tell us about, anything that we haven't asked you that you feel we should, or anything else that you would like to add in defence of your thesis? You don't have to say anything, but this is your opportunity to do so before you leave us'.

Jonathan thinks a little, looks at Dr Forest, and then thinks again. He has enjoyed the discussion, and feels that it was fair, but can't think of anything to say. He feels he should say something: 'No, I don't have anything to add. I would just like to thank the examiners for taking the time to read my work, and coming here today to examine me.'

Jonathan and Dr Forest leave the room and return to Dr Forest's office to wait to be called back and told the outcome.

The time is now 12.15pm.

6.5 The private meeting post-viva

A buffet lunch has arrived for the examination panel, and the examiners help themselves to some food. They begin to discuss Jonathan's performance in the viva.

Professor Turns starts the discussion: 'Well, colleagues, how do you think he performed during the viva? Derek, can I ask you to start as the external examiner, please?'

Professor Koyne: 'I thought he performed very well. It's clear that he understands the work, and that he has done it. I still have some concerns about the areas I talked about this morning, but overall I am confident that he has reached the necessary standard. I do think some revisions are needed to the thesis'.

Professor Turns: 'And Susan, your view please?'

Dr West: 'I agree. I enjoyed the discussion and I thought he did very well. I think that he should pass, but that he does need to make some changes to the thesis to bring it fully up to standard'.

Professor Turns: 'Good. It seems we are in agreement that the candidate should pass, subject to some revisions to the thesis. The next question is whether these should be termed minor amendments or major amendments'.

Professor Koyne: 'What do your regulations say about that?'

Professor Turns consults his copy of the regulations: 'According to our university regulations, minor amendments are normally typos and very small changes to the text, and must be completed within three months.

Major amendments are more significant changes to the thesis, and the candidate is given up to six months to complete them. Perhaps it would help if we talked about the nature of the amendments that we are going to ask for. That might help us decide whether these are best termed major or minor amendments. Can we do that please?'

Professor Koyne: 'Yes that's fine. As a minimum I would want him to rewrite the abstract, explain a little more about his methodological approach, and add a little to the evaluation chapter. I also feel he needs to say a little more about how he actually analysed the data; and that should probably come in Chapter 5. I think he answered my other questions fine, and I thus wouldn't require any further changes. I did spot quite a few typos and I've marked them on my copy, which I am happy for him to take away with him."

Dr West: 'I agree with all of that. I would also like Jonathan to reconsider his research questions, and perhaps reformulate them. I don't want to be prescriptive about that, after all it's his thesis. But I do think that he should at least consider them again. Oh, and there are a lot of acronyms and terms which aren't properly defined. I think he needs to add a glossary of terms, and of course he also needs to correct those figures in Chapter 5. I also feel that his concluding chapter could be strengthened to emphasise the contribution to knowledge and the implications for practice and policy. He hasn't said anything substantial about the limitations of his work, and I asked him about that. His answer was OK, but I think he needs to add a little to the final chapter, and return to his questions. Oh, and he has to sort his references. I've also marked up my copy of the thesis and he can take that away with him. I've gone through the reference list and marked any inconsistencies that I spotted. The university provides some excellent training on stuff like referencing which he must have attended, and we give them some software, so he really should be able to sort them out'.

Professor Turns: 'This sounds like borderline between minor and major amendments to me. I sit on our university research degrees committee and we sometimes spend ages discussing whether amendments are major or minor. I think I would veer towards calling them major, because there is quite a bit more than simple typos here. That would also give him six months in which to do them. Of course, he doesn't have to take the full six months, but at least it's there if he needs it. What do you think?'

Professor Koyne and Dr West both agree.

Professor Turns: 'The next thing we need to decide is who is going read the revised thesis and sign off the changes. This can either by Susan, as internal examiner, or both of you. Derek, would you wish to see the amended thesis?'

Professor Koyne: 'No. I'm quite happy for Susan to sign them off. I would like a final copy of the thesis for my book shelf. I think he has done a good piece of work, and his thesis could be of use to some of my students. I'll ask him if he can provide me with a copy of the final thesis'.

Professor Turns: 'That's great. Many thanks to both of you. It looks like we have a way forward. We also have a form to complete. Should we do that now before we ask them back in?'

Professor Koyne: 'Yes let's do that'.

The examiners now complete the official form which details the outcome that they are recommending to the university. Their recommendation will need to be approved by the university before it is confirmed and sent to the candidate; it will normally be discussed by a committee, such as the research degrees committee. Figure 6.4 (pp. 105–107) presents an example form.

Professor Turns: 'I'll read each of the questions. First, does the thesis represent a significant contribution to knowledge of the subject by the discovery of new facts and/or the exercise of independent critical powers?'

Professor Koyne: 'Yes, I think we are all clear that the work makes a contribution, and yes, there has been the discovery of some new facts'.

Dr West: 'And there is clear evidence of critical thinking; so yes from me to all of that'.

Professor Turns: 'Does the thesis provide evidence of originality?'

Professor Koyne and Dr West together: 'Yes'.

Professor Turns:' Is the thesis satisfactory as regards literary presentation and succinctness?'

Professor Koyne: 'I think we have to say 'no' to this question, as there are a few things that need sorting out'.

Professor Turns: 'Is the abstract of the thesis submitted acceptable?'

Dr West: 'I think we need to say 'no' to this question too, as we both felt that the abstract needs to be improved before the final thesis is lodged with the library'.

Professor Turns: 'Thank you. We now need to make a comment on the thesis'.

The examiners discuss and agree a short statement which highlights the positive aspects of Jonathan's thesis, including the opinion that it makes a contribution to knowledge. They also include references to some of the areas that they feel need improving in the revised version.

Professor Turns: 'We now have to answer some questions about Jonathan's performance in the viva. Are we satisfied that the thesis presented is the candidate's own work?'

Both examiners: 'Yes, definitely'.

Professor Turns: 'Did the candidate show a satisfactory knowledge and understanding of matters relating to the thesis, and background studies to the subject of the thesis?'

Professor Koyne: 'Yes on both counts. I thought he performed very well and clearly understands the literature which surrounds his own work.'

Professor Turns: 'Thank you. We now need to make a comment on his performance in the viva'.

The examiners discuss and agree a short statement which indicates that Jonathan did well during the viva.

Professor Turns: 'Thank you. Finally, we need to make record the outcome of the examination on the form. I think you have agreed that we will make the following recommendation:

CONDITIONAL PASS with Major Amendments: That the candidate be recommended for the degree of PhD subject to amendments being made to the thesis to the satisfaction of the Internal Examiner only.

Is that OK?'

The examiners look at each other, nod in agreement and Professor Turns ticks the appropriate box on the form.

Professor Turns: 'All that leaves now is the list of amendments. Shall we complete that by email later? We can do so and then attach it to the form. Are you both OK with that?'

The examiners agree to making up the list of corrections in this way. They all sign the form. They subsequently exchange emails, with Professor Koyne starting with a draft list. Dr West adds to the list, and changes a few points. Professor Turns then formats the final list and appends it to the final form, which he submits to the Graduate School Office, who put it on the agenda of the next Research Degrees Committee. The final agreed list of amendments is presented in Figure 6.5 (p. 108).

Professor Turns: 'Good. I'd better go and get Jonathan. Who should tell him the outcome?'

Professor Koyne: 'Oh I think you should as Chair'.

Professor Turns goes to collect Jonathan from Dr Forest's office.

The time is now 12.55pm.

6.6 Relaying the outcome to the candidate

Jonathan and Dr Forest have been waiting for 40 minutes and are both very anxious. For Jonathan it has been the longest 40 minutes of his life. Many different thoughts are running through his head. Why are they taking so long? What are they talking about? Have I failed? Are they going to ask me to do more work? All of these thoughts are pretty irrational actually, given the way the viva went, but that doesn't stop them popping up in Jonathan's mind. Dr Forest tries to reassure him. He has been an observer in several of his students' vivas, and he feels that Jonathan's viva went well, so he is expecting a positive outcome. However, that doesn't stop him worrying either.

Recommendation of the Examiners on a candidate for the degree of Doctor of Philosophy

The Examiners are required, where possible to complete a joint report on this form on the thesis, oral or alternative examination, the result of the examination as a whole and the recommendation to the University.

1. THE CANDIDATE

Name:	Jonathan Foxton
Department:	Archaeology
Title of thesis:	An investigation into Y
Supervisor:	Dr Forest
Date of Examination:	7th January 2013

2. THE EXAMINATION BOARD

External Examiner(s):	Professor Derek Koyne
Internal Examiner:	Dr Susan West
Independent Chair:	Professor Keith Turns
Supervisor present:	Dr Brian Forest was present

3. REPORT OF THE EXAMINERS ON THE THESIS

The Examiners are requested to give a reasoned assessment of the candidate's performance.

	YES	NO
3.1 Does the thesis represent a significant contribution to knowledge of the subject by:		
(i) The discovery of new facts?	☑	☐
and/or		
(ii) The exercise of independent critical powers?	☑	☐
3.2 Does the thesis provide evidence of originality?	☑	☐
3.3 Is the thesis satisfactory as regards literary presentation and succinctness?	☐	☑
3.4 Is the abstract of the thesis submitted acceptable?	☐	☑

3.5 Comments on the thesis:

The thesis presents a clear contribution to knowledge in the subject. The methodological approach is sound, but would benefit from a little more justification in the thesis. The research questions could be a little clearer and more precise. The study produces some interesting results which have been discussed well. The thesis covers the relevant literature and demonstrates critical evaluation. The thesis is well-structured, and in general well-written; however, there are a number of typographical errors which will need correcting in the final version. The abstract of the thesis does not fully represent the excellent work that has been done and should be rewritten to reflect what has been done and to highlight the contribution made by the work. The thesis does not fully express the evaluation which the candidate has undertaken.

Figure 6.4 The recommendation form (*continued overleaf*)

4. REPORT OF THE EXAMINERS ON THE ORAL EXAMINATION

The Examiners are requested to report below on the oral examination of the candidate giving a reasoned assessment of the candidate's performance.

	YES	NO	N/A
4.1 Are you satisfied that the thesis presented is the candidate's own work?	☑	☐	
4.2 Did the candidate show a satisfactory knowledge and understanding of:			
(i) matters relating to the thesis?	☑	☐	
(ii) background studies to the subject of the thesis?	☑	☐	
4.3 In the case of a candidate whose research programme was part of a collaborative group project, did the oral examination demonstrate that the candidate's own contribution was worthy of the award?	☐	☐	☑

Comments on the oral examination

The candidate defended his thesis well. He responded to all questions and engaged in a useful and interesting discussion with the examiners. The candidate is to be congratulated on his performance during the viva.

The viva addressed the areas of research questions, methodology and evaluation. These are all areas which the examiners felt could be made clearer in the thesis. The candidate addressed the examiners' concerns in each of these areas, and they are of the view that they can be rectified by revisions to the final thesis.

Overall the examiners are satisfied that the candidate has reached doctoral level.

5. RECOMMENDATION

If the examiners recommendations are not in agreement, a separate form should be completed by each individual examiner to evidence that a detailed assessment of the thesis has been carried out and to clarify the differences in the judgements made.

The examiners are requested to tick one recommendation only:

5.1 PASS

☐ That the candidate be recommended for the degree of PhD.

5.2a CONDITIONAL PASS (Minor Amendments)

☐ That the candidate be recommended for the degree of PhD subject to corrections being made to the thesis to the satisfaction of the internal examiner

5.2b CONDITIONAL PASS (Major Amendments)

That the candidate be recommended for the degree of PhD subject to amendments being made to the thesis to the satisfaction of the:

☐ Internal Examiner(s) and External Examiner(s)

☑ Internal Examiner(s) only

☐ External Examiner(s) only

It is expected that the candidate should normally complete minor amendments within 3 months and major amendments within 6 months.

Figure 6.4 *continued* The recommendation form

5.3 REFERRAL FOR PHD

That the candidate be permitted to re-submit for the degree of PhD and be re-examined as follows (*as specified by the Examiners*)

☐ (i) *the thesis must be revised and, if deemed satisfactory by the Examiners, the candidate will be exempt from further examination, oral or otherwise;

☐ (ii) *the thesis must be revised and the candidate must undergo a further oral or alternative examination;

Where the examiners recommend that the candidate should re-submit for PhD, a list of deficiencies of the thesis must be detailed in section 6. The revised thesis must be submitted for re-examination within one year.

5.4 OFFER AWARD OF MPhil

☐ That the candidate meets the criteria for the award of MPhil but not those of PhD, therefore the degree of MPhil should be granted.

5.5 NO DEGREE AWARDED

☐ That no award be made

6. GUIDANCE FROM THE EXAMINERS FOLLOWING THE EXAMINATION FOR THE DEGREE OF PHD

(a) Details of any amendments to the thesis should be detailed below.

List to follow.

(b) Where the thesis was found to be unsatisfactory on the first examination, the Examiners are asked to provide guidance for candidates who will be required to undertake a re-examination, this should include guidance on the structure and content of the thesis.

(c) Where appropriate the examiners are asked to indicate the nature of any other deficiencies in the candidate's performance in the oral and/or other examination.

Examiners: Signed *Professor Derek Koyne*   Date *7th January 2013*

Signed *Dr Susan West*   Date *7th January 2013*

All examiners should sign this form. The Independent Chair should forward the form to the Graduate Research School office promptly after the examination.

Independent Chair

I confirm that the examination was conducted in accordance with the University Regulations for the Award of Doctor of Philosophy.

Signed *Professor Keith Turns*   Date *7th January 2013*

Amendments required to the thesis

Jonathan Foxton

The abstract of the thesis should be rewritten to more clearly describe the work done, including reference to the theoretical contexts explored and the contribution made by the research.

Provide a Glossary of Terms (acronyms in particular) used in the thesis. This should appear after the Table of Contents. Also, within the main body of the thesis, always provide the full meaning of an acronym, the first time each is used.

Chapter 1. Review and refine your research questions. Consider reducing the number of questions, and ensure that they are precise, to reflect the discussions with the examiners during the viva.

Chapter 3. Methodology. Justify your methodological approach with reference to the literature and explain how you used the methods in practice. If you adapted published methods to fit your own study, say this, and explain why.

Chapter 5. Explain how you analysed the data. This can be relatively brief. One or two paragraphs will suffice. Ensure that all figures and in particular Figures 5.6 to 5.9 are properly and clearly labelled and that every figure is referred to and discussed within the main body of the text.

Chapter 7. Evaluation. Add a page or two which compares your work to that of other researchers in the field.

The concluding chapter should emphasise the original contribution to knowledge made by the thesis in relation to the body of academic literature; and also the implications for practice and policy. Limitations of the study as a whole should be identified in terms of scope, theory and methodology. Return to your research questions. Has your study fully answered them?

Ensure that all the references cited in the thesis are referenced correctly in the text and included in the reference list at the end of the thesis. For example, Craig et al., cited as 2002 in the thesis on page 56 (the first entry), is referenced as both 2001(a) and 2001(b) in the reference list. Make sure that you are consistent and adhere to Harvard style throughout.

Revise the thesis to correct any typographical errors. Both examiners have provided their annotated copies of the thesis in order to highlight specific errors. These will also help the candidate to complete the revision of the thesis in light of the comments above.

Figure 6.5 List of amendments

Professor Turns pops his head around the door: 'Right Jonathan. We are ready for you'. Professor Turns seems to be smiling, which reassures Jonathan that perhaps all may be well after all. They walk to the viva room; Professor Turns doesn't speak. He feels that he has to wait until he is back in the room with the examiners before he can relay the good news to Jonathan and his supervisor. The walk to the room only takes a minute or two, but for Jonathan it seems to take for ever.

They reach the examination room. The examiners are also smiling.

Professor Turns: 'Welcome back Jonathan, and thanks for waiting for us. I am pleased to be able to tell you that my colleagues were impressed by your thesis and your performance in the viva this morning, and that they are recommending that you Pass and be awarded your PhD, subject to some revisions to the thesis. Congratulations, Dr Foxton'.

The examiners all congratulate Jonathan. He shakes hands with everyone. It's all a bit of a blur; he can't believe he has finally got to this point and that the news is so good.

Professor Turns: 'Jonathan, I should also tell you that this outcome is a recommendation to the university, and that the Research Degrees Committee will need to consider and approve the examiners' recommendation. I should also say something about the amendments, as there are quite a few of them. You'll receive a full list of amendments from the Graduate Research School shortly. The amendments cover the sort of areas that the examiners discussed with you during the viva: your research question, methodology and evaluation. And there are also quite a few typos which you'll need to sort out in the final version of your thesis. Oh, and the referencing needs fully checking and correcting, using Harvard style throughout. As I say, your examiners will produce a list and you'll get this from the Graduate Research School in due course. As I hope you appreciate, they are asking you to make these revisions so that the final thesis is something that we can all be proud of, and that will do you justice when it is placed in the library and available for everyone to read. The amendments will need to be done to Dr West's satisfaction. You will be given 6 months to do them, but you don't have to take that long. They shouldn't take you too long to do'.

Jonathan nods. It's a lot to take in. But the important thing is they used the word PASS, so he can relax now. And those changes don't seem too bad anyway.

The examiners both give Jonathan their marked up copy of the thesis, and he returns to his desk in the research office, laden with the heavy documents, but pleased and very relieved. He rings his friends and family to tell them of the outcome.

6.7 After the day of the viva

Jonathan doesn't hear anything about the viva for a few weeks after the day of the examination. Professor Turns emails the entire department to congratulate Jonathan, and everyone is calling him 'Dr', although he feels a bit of a fraud because the degree hasn't yet been fully awarded. (Actually, the title 'Dr' should be used officially only after the degree has been formally confirmed by the university's research degrees committee or the equivalent awarding body.)

Professor Turns emails Jonathan the list of amendments so that he can start revising his thesis while he is awaiting the formal notification from the university. He eventually receives a letter from the Graduate Research School, confirming the outcome of his examination (see Figure 6.6).

Jonathan spent two months making the revisions to his thesis. He felt that they were pretty straightforward, and the list provided by the examiners was quite clear and specific. He also went through the marked-up copies of the thesis and made sure that he made all the typographical corrections that they had indicated, and any that he found himself. He was surprised how many there were. He got a little confused when consulting Professor Koyne's copy of the thesis. Professor Koyne had written quite a few additional comments, and some of his questions, on the pages, and these confused Jonathan; he wasn't sure what to do in response to these, and indeed if he should do anything at all with them. However, he discussed this with Dr Forest and between them they were able to work out which were questions

---

Dear Jonathan

PhD Examination

Following your recent *viva voce* examination, the Examiners made the following recommendation:

"that the candidate be recommended for the award of the degree of PhD, subject to amendments being made to the thesis, to the satisfaction of Internal Examiner".

I am pleased to confirm that the University Research Degrees Committee has approved the recommendation of the examiners. Please find attached a copy of the 'Recommendation of the Examiners on a Candidate for the Degree of Doctor of Philosophy' form completed by the examiners, for your information. Please also find attached the list of amendments required to your thesis.

Please note that the University Regulations for the Award of Doctor of Philosophy state that amendments to the thesis should be completed within a maximum of 6 months from the date of approval of the recommendation by the Research Degrees Committee. When you have completed the amendments you should submit one soft bound copy of the thesis to this office for the consideration of the internal examiner.

If you have any queries, please do not hesitate to contact me.

Well done in your examination and many congratulations.

Best wishes

Laura

Graduate Research School Office
University of Neverland

Figure 6.6 Letter of formal notification of the outcome of the examination

and which were things he should correct in the final version. Professor Koyne emailed Dr Forest with a copy of the paper as promised, so Jonathan was able to consider the implications of that, and include some additional comparisons within his thesis.

When Jonathan was finished he printed off a final draft copy and gave it to Dr Forest for a final check. Dr Forest found a couple of further typos and made some comments on the additional material relating to evaluation. Jonathan responded to these, printed off the final version and submitted it to the Graduate Research School office. It took a little time, probably a further month, before he received a letter confirming that Dr West had approved the thesis, and that he now had to prepare the final bound version of the thesis. This was accompanied by a booklet outlining lots of formatting instructions telling him how to lay out the cover, margins and so on. Once he had produced the final bound copy, he received a further letter confirming award of the degree and inviting him to the next graduation ceremony, which was three months away. He received his certificate from the registry a month before the ceremony.

Jonathan enjoyed his day at the graduation ceremony. Dr Forest accompanied him on stage to formally receive his PhD. It was a wonderful experience; everyone was very proud of Jonathan, and he had a great time celebrating his success.

Jonathan kept his promise of publishing a paper from his thesis. In fact, in preparing the paper it became clear that the work would be better framed as two papers, both of which were co-authored with Dr Forest. They were eventually published, after some revisions, in two well-respected journals. The process took longer than Jonathan expected; there was almost one year between his examination and his work appearing in a journal.

6.8 Alternative models for the viva

This chapter has simulated a viva within the UK system. In other countries the nature of the viva may be quite different. In particular, some countries operate a public viva system. The constitution of the panel may also have some differences. However, the format of a pre-meeting, followed by the viva itself and a private discussion between the examiners before relaying a provisional recommendation to the candidate is likely to be the same. You will need to check this with your own university.

6.9 Discussion

This chapter has presented a simulation of a viva. As I stated in my health warning at the start of the chapter, you must treat this purely as an example to illustrate the viva process. It is not possible to predict the actual questions which you will experience during your own viva. I have tried to indicate some of the possible types of question that might arise, and how the candidate dealt with these in this case. I have also given examples of the sort of views and issues that examiners can bring with them to a viva.

There are a number of points which I wanted to illustrate within this chapter, including:

- It is all right to ask the examiner to repeat a question if you are unsure of exactly what is being asked.
- It is acceptable to take your time and think about your answer.
- You may be asked to explain some areas of your work in significant detail. In this example, the candidate was asked to explain some parts of his work by writing on the whiteboard. Don't be afraid of this; you will understand the work that you have done and you will have no problem in going into detail.
- An examiner may raise something which you hadn't considered, and it is acceptable to agree with that point and to incorporate it into the final version of your thesis.
- It is good to recognise and be prepared to discuss the limitations of your work.
- The examiners may take what seems a long time in their private meeting before and/or after the viva. This is normal, so don't worry. It doesn't necessarily mean that they have a big problem with your work – they have a lot to talk about and various pieces of documentation to complete, which all takes time.
- The process has several stages: submitting your thesis; arranging the viva; receiving a formal list of amendments; and receiving formal notification of the outcome from the university. All of these stages take quite some time.

As I have explained on a number of occasions, the viva is a vital and integral part of the entire PhD assessment process. Sometimes an examiner may come along to a viva with a number of issues, and a number of areas where they feel the thesis requires revision. However, if these are fully addressed by the candidate during the viva, the examiner may no longer feel the revisions are needed. This will depend on the nature of the issues. Clearly, if there are things within the thesis which are incorrect, these must be put right in the final copy of the thesis. Students often don't do themselves justice within the thesis; a good external examiner will draw out the positives of the work during the viva.

Summary

This chapter has simulated an entire viva. I hope that you have found it interesting to read, and that it is useful in illustrating some of the processes involved. As I stressed at the start of the chapter, it is not possible to predict the questions that will be asked in your own viva, or how it might play out. However, I hope that this fictional viva has helped you to get a better idea of how a viva works, the stages that are involved, and what happens during each stage. I have also included some typical documentation so that you can see the type of forms that the examiners need to complete in doing their job. The documentation should be treated as an illustration; each university will have their own forms. You will be able to obtain copies of the forms, should you wish to see them, from the relevant office (for example, the Graduate Research School office or the Registry). The next chapter covers in detail all the possible outcomes that may result from a viva, and discusses how you might deal with each of them.

7 The Outcome

On completion of this chapter you will:

▶ understand all of the possible outcomes that may result from your viva

▶ be in a better position to react to any of those possible outcome

7.1 Chapter overview

The viva can result in several possible outcomes, ranging from a straight Pass, through various levels of amendments and revisions to re-submission, the award of MPhil or (very rarely) outright Fail. Each of these possible outcomes is discussed in some detail, with reference to university regulations and documentation. The questions which are often asked of examiners on the assessment documentation are used as an illustration. The chapter covers how to take the next steps after the outcome of your viva has been decided, including how to approach amendments, further work or a further examination. Appeal processes and the grounds on which a candidate might appeal are also discussed. Recovering from the viva and the sense of achievement, mixed with a feeling of anti-climax which candidates often report, are covered.

I allude to the role of your supervisor and others in supporting you in making changes to the thesis, or in doing further work. The importance of precision in addressing the comments of the examiners, and how to deal with any lack of clarity in this, is also covered.

Hartley and Jory (2000) studied the viva experiences of candidates and found that the majority of students were physically drained as they came out of the viva. However, they also felt uplifted (although, for obvious reasons, this varied depending upon the outcome). The majority of candidates felt that their viva was a positive experience: 64% expressed a boost of morale and 75% were positive about their examiners.

"On the day of the viva I met my supervisor and she came into the viva with me for support. My viva lasted for two hours and afterwards I had to wait outside for a few minutes (which seemed like an eternity). Then I was asked to return to the room with my supervisor and given the good news that I had passed, with some minor corrections. After hearing the good news, the examiners did talk to me, but to be honest I can't remember a thing!"

7.2 Possible outcomes

There are several possible outcomes of the viva, which the examination panel will recommend to the university. Although these may vary from one university to another they will usually include the following possible recommendations:

- Pass with no corrections.
- Pass with minor amendments (typographical errors and small changes to the thesis).
- Pass with major amendments (re-drafting or the addition of sections or chapters)
- Re-submission of the work (more research to be undertaken or a major re-write of the thesis).
- Not a pass at doctoral level but an award of a Master's degree may be offered.
- Fail, and no degree awarded, with no further opportunity for assessment.

The next parts of this section cover each of these outcomes, and what you should do in each case. I start each part with the relevant extract from some sample university regulations.

"When I embarked on the programme, I had no clear expectations other than I wanted to see if I could achieve at this level of academic work. I can honestly say that, if my work resulted in a fail, whilst I would naturally be disappointed, I could walk away knowing that I have personally developed in a way that I never anticipated."

7.2.1 Pass with no corrections

PASS: *That the candidate be recommended for the degree of PhD.*

This outcome is quite rare. In the 100 or so vivas I have attended I can count on one hand the number of students who have passed without any changes at all to their thesis. It is quite unusual for the examiner to find no small ty-pographical errors, and nothing that they feel needs to be changed. It is now so easy to make any small corrections with the use of a word-processing package that examiners don't worry about asking a candidate to make some small changes to their thesis. So if you do pass without any changes at all to your thesis, then well done! You can truly celebrate immediately after the viva. All that will be left to do will be to prepare a final hard-bound copy of your thesis for the library.

7.2.2   Pass with minor amendments

CONDITIONAL PASS (Minor Amendments): That the candidate be recommended for the degree of PhD subject to corrections being made to the thesis to the satisfaction of the internal examiner.

It is expected that the candidate should normally complete minor amendments within 3 months and major amendments within 6 months.

This is probably the most common outcome. This means that the examiners feel everything is at the correct standard, that you performed well in the viva, and that in general your thesis is acceptable. However, there are some small amendments such as typographical errors, headings on figures or referencing issues which must be addressed in the final version of your thesis. This may also include adding a sentence or two of additional explanation in a few places. You will be allowed a short period of time to correct these (normally one, two or three months, depending upon the regulations of your university) and they will normally need to be approved by the internal examiner only.

If this is the outcome of your viva, do the amendments to your thesis as quickly as you are able. Ask your supervisor to run a quick check of them, and then submit the final version of your thesis to the university, who will send it to the internal examiner for approval. As long as you have done what you have been asked, the degree will then be awarded.

7.2.3   Pass with major amendments

CONDITIONAL PASS (Major Amendments): That the candidate be recommended for the degree of PhD subject to amendments being made to the thesis to the satisfaction of the:

☐ *Internal Examiner(s) and External Examiner(s)*

☐ *Internal Examiner(s) only*

☐ *External Examiner(s) only*

It is expected that the candidate should normally complete minor amendments within 3 months and major amendments within 6 months.

This regulation is relatively new, and not every university includes it. In this case, the examiners are basically saying that you have reached the correct standard, that your work makes a contribution and that you performed adequately during the viva. However, there are areas of your thesis which require improvement and these changes are more than minor amendments. A pass with major amendments will usually involve the addition of sections of explanation or additional discussion to the thesis, and it may also involve the reordering or restructuring of chapters. It is unlikely to involve the collection of new data or the need to undertake further research, other than perhaps reading some additional literature that the examiners feel was missing, and should be included in your thesis. You will be allowed a longer period of time to fulfil these amendments (normally six months, depending upon the regulations of your university) and the examiners will decide, and inform you, who is to approve them. This may be the internal examiner or both the internal and the external examiner. The examiners will provide you with a list of the amendments that you are required to make.

If this is the outcome of your viva, you are likely to experience some mixed emotions. On the one hand, you have (almost) passed, but on the other, the examiners are requiring quite a bit of change to your thesis. The best thing to do is to get on with the changes straight away. In my experience, very few students in this position have needed to take the full six months that they were allowed in order to complete the changes. Ask your supervisor to advise you on the amendments you are making, and work carefully through the list of things that you are required to do, making sure that you fully address all of them. When you have done so, produce a list of the amendments that you have made, and where they are to be found in your thesis. This will help the examiner(s) to quickly check that you have covered everything that they asked of you. An example of such a list is provided as an example in Figure 7.1, which shows how the candidate in

Amendments to PhD thesis: Jonathan Foxton	
REQUIREMENT	HOW AND WHERE ADDRESSED IN THE THESIS
The abstract of the thesis should be rewritten to more clearly describe the work done, including reference to the theoretical contexts explored and the contribution made by the research.	The abstract has been completely rewritten to take account of the recommendations of the examiners, and the changes made to the thesis.
Provide a Glossary of Terms (acronyms in particular) used in the thesis. This should appear after the Table of Contents. Also, within the main body of the thesis, always provide the full meaning of an acronym, the first time each is used.	A Glossary of Terms is included at the start of the thesis and can be found at page vi. Within the main body of the thesis the full meaning of each acronym is given the first time it is used.
Chapter 1. Review and refine your research questions. Consider reducing the number of questions, and ensure that they are precise, to reflect the discussions with the examiners during the viva.	The research questions have been reformulated to improve clarity and precision, and remove duplication. The new questions can be found on page 12.

Figure 7.1 Sample list of amendments to Jonathan's PhD thesis, showing how he addressed the requirements of the examiners (*continued overleaf*)

REQUIREMENT	HOW AND WHERE ADDRESSED IN THE THESIS
Chapter 3. Methodology. Justify your methodological approach with reference to the literature and explain how you used the methods in practice. If you adapted published methods to fit your own study, say this, and explain why.	Chapter 3 has been revised to justify the methodological approach (pages 52–55) and more detail is included about how the methods were applied (pages 62–71).
Chapter 5. Explain how you analysed the data. This can be relatively brief. One or two paragraphs will suffice. Ensure that all figures, and in particular Figures 5.6 to 5.9, are properly and clearly labelled and that every figure is referred to and discussed within the main body of the text.	A section has been added to Chapter 5 (page 98) to explain how the data were analysed. All figures have been checked; they are now all correctly labelled and are all referred to within the body of the text.
Chapter 7. Evaluation. Add a page or two which compares your work to that of other researchers in the field.	A section has been added to Chapter 7 which compares my work to that of other researchers (pages 154–155).
The concluding chapter should emphasise the original contribution to knowledge made by the thesis in relation to the body of academic literature; and also the implications for practice and policy. Limitations of the study as a whole should be identified in terms of scope, theory and methodology. Return to your research questions. Has your study fully answered them?	A section has been added to the last chapter entitled 'Contribution to Knowledge' (pages 182–184). Sections have been added to discuss the implications for policy and practice, and the limitations of the study (pages 185–187). The research questions have been returned to (pages 189–190).
Ensure that all the references cited in the thesis are referenced correctly in the text and included in the reference list at the end of the thesis. For example, Craig et al., cited as 2002 in the thesis on page 56 (the first entry), is referenced as both 2001(a) and 2001(b) in the reference list. Make sure that you are consistent and adhere to Harvard style throughout.	The references have been fully checked. They are all correctly cited and the reference list is in standard Harvard format, as required by the university regulations.
Revise the thesis to correct any typographical errors. Both examiners have provided their annotated copies of the thesis in order to highlight specific errors. These will also help the candidate complete the revision of the thesis in light of the comments above.	The thesis has been fully checked. All typographical errors as indicated on the examiners' copies of the thesis have been corrected along with those identified by the candidate and his supervisor.

Figure 7.1 *continued*

the previous chapter addressed the points which the examiners raised. Ask your supervisor to look over these, and then submit the final version of your thesis to the university who will send it to the examiner(s) for approval. You will have to wait a little time before you hear back from the university (perhaps a month or two), but as long as you have done what you have been asked, the degree will be awarded.

7.2.4   Re-submission

REFERRAL FOR PHD: That the candidate be permitted to re-submit for the degree of PhD and be re-examined as follows (*as specified by the examiners):

☐ *(i)   *the thesis must be revised and if deemed satisfactory by the examiners, the candidate will be exempt from further examination, oral or otherwise;*

☐ *(ii) *the thesis must be revised and the candidate must undergo a further oral or alternative examination.*

Where the examiners recommend that the candidate should re-submit for PhD, a list of deficiencies of the thesis must be detailed. The revised thesis must be submitted for re-examination within one year.

If this is the outcome of your viva you will no doubt be extremely disappointed. This outcome is not very common, but does happen. It indicates that the examiners feel there are major deficiencies in the thesis, and may also indicate that they feel that the candidate needs to do further work (such as collecting further data, or performing further experiments) before doctoral standard is reached. However, in every case where this happened and I have personally been involved as a supervisor, examiner or Chair, the candidate has ultimately re-submitted their thesis and passed. You will be given very clear advice by the examiners as to the deficiencies of your initial submission, and what they feel you need to do in order to raise the work to the required standard.

As you can see from the short regulation extract above, the examiners will have two choices. First, if they feel that your performance in the viva has been satisfactory, they may decide that no further viva is required. This means that you are required to revise and re-submit your thesis, but you won't need to attend a further oral examination. The regulations usually, however, allow the examiners to hold a viva 'in reserve'. If, when you re-submit your thesis, the examiners feel that there are some issues which are unclear or need further discussion they may decide to call you for a viva after all.

The second option which the examiners may choose is that you are re-quired to re-submit your thesis and to attend for a further viva. There may be two reasons for this. The examiners may feel that you did not perform adequately during the first viva; perhaps you were not able to discuss and defend your work well enough, or perhaps you did not demonstrate suffi-cient knowledge of the literature or methodology. Alternatively, the exam-iners may feel that the revisions to the thesis are so substantial that they will, in effect, be examining a new thesis (or at least a thesis with some significant new aspects). As a result, it will be sensible (and potentially to your advantage) to hold a second viva so that they have the opportunity to discuss the revised (new) work with you.

If you are in the position described here, the first thing you must do is discuss the situation with your supervisor. Unless you have submitted with-out taking all of their advice into account, they will be just as shocked and disappointed as you. They wouldn't have suggested that you go forward to viva unless they thought that you had a good chance of success. However, peer review by the examiners has revealed some areas which they feel need addressing and/or some further work which you need to do. The first thing to do, unless you feel that something has gone terribly wrong (and I will cover the subject of how to lodge an appeal against an examination deci-sion later in this chapter), is to accept their judgement. The examiners will have considered your performance in the viva and your thesis very carefully and will not have come to this decision lightly.

I have known several students in this situation who have talked of quit-ting. This is understandable because a result like this comes as a huge dis-appointment. However, in all cases the student has decided to continue, to do the additional work and to re-submit for the degree. To do anything else would be a great shame, and a waste of all the time and effort which you have put into the work to date. In every instance, the candidate has picked themselves up, engaged with the process, and has ultimately passed and been awarded their PhD. And, in most cases, they have over time recog-nised that the additional work has strengthened their thesis, and understood why the examiners required them to do it.

Having accepted the decision, you now need to make a plan to address the required work. You should discuss the list of requirements provided by the examiners with your supervisor. Make sure that you understand every aspect of it and see exactly what the examiners require. You may have been provided with some quite specific things to do. However, and particularly if you need to do some further research, you may have some choices to make because there may be several possible routes forward in order to address the issues that the examiners have raised. If there are some things which you and your supervisor feel are not clear, it may be possible to go back to the examiners and ask them to explain the requirements in more detail. This must be done through the university in a formal way; either through the Chair of your examination panel or through your Graduate Research School office or equivalent (who will be able to advise you on this).

When you and your supervisor are confident that you fully understand what is required of you, produce a plan to complete the work in the period allowed (normally one year). It may be tempting to try and do the work as quickly as possible. I would urge you to take your time, not to rush the additional work, and to give it the attention that it deserves. In this situation the additional work required is usually substantial, and you need to take the time to consider it carefully. Your supervisor should help you with this, and read and comment upon your revised thesis as it develops.

When the revised thesis is ready, submit it to the university, who will send it to the examiners for their consideration. It is important that you and your supervisor are satisfied with the additional work that you have done, and that it has reached the required standard because a further re-submission will not be allowed. The only outcomes available to the examiners now will be Pass (perhaps with some amendments, depending on your university regulations), award a Master's degree, or Fail.

7.2.5   Award of a Master's degree

OFFER AWARD OF MPhil: *That the candidate meets the criteria for the award of MPhil but not those of PhD, therefore the degree of MPhil should be granted.*

This outcome is very rare, but can, and does sometimes, happen. In this case, the examiners are of the opinion that the work is not of doctoral standard and that a Master's award should be offered to the candidate. This may be as a result of a re-submission, in which case the examiners are not allowed to give the candidate a further attempt at PhD. Or it may be on first attempt, if the examiners are of the opinion that the work (or the candidate) could never reach doctoral standard. Some university regulations will only allow the award of a Master's degree after a re-submission (that is, a candidate has, in effect, the right to a re-submission on first attempt). In some universities, the award of a lower degree must be an *offer* to the candidate (that is, the candidate has, on first attempt, the right to refuse the offer and to opt for a re-submission, even if this is against the advice of the examiners).

This situation involves the offer of a lower award, and not the award for which the candidate was registered. The UK QAA Quality Code (2011) is very clear that 'qualifications should be awarded to mark the achievement of positively defined outcomes, not as compensation for failure at a higher level, or by default'. The Code goes on to state that 'failure at a higher level does not mean that a lower qualification cannot be awarded ... a lower qualification should only be awarded if the student has demonstrated the outcomes required for that qualification.' In other words, the examiners are required to assess your thesis and performance in the viva against the standards for a Master's award, and should only make that award if they are confident that Master's standard has been achieved. This may require that you make some changes to the thesis to ensure that it does satisfy the requirements of a Masters award.

If you are in this position, you must check very carefully the options that are open to you and discuss them with your supervisor. I do know of candidates who have been awarded a Master's degree and have subsequently registered for a new PhD programme. These candidates ultimately, after three years' further study, achieved a PhD.

7.2.6 Fail

NO DEGREE AWARDED: *That no award be made, and the candidate be given no further opportunity to re-submit the thesis for the award of the degree.*

This is a very rare outcome, and usually only happens after the candidate has been allowed a re-submission. The system of annual reviews of progress and reviews of the thesis by the supervisor should guard against this happening, and should not allow a candidate to progress to viva unless they have a reasonable chance of success. Students whose research is not progressing well will often withdraw from their studies at an earlier stage, or be required to withdraw by their university. I am pleased to say that, in all of the examinations which I have been involved in any capacity, I have never experienced a candidate who has failed at this, the final hurdle. If a candidate is not likely to succeed, for whatever reason, it is unlikely that they will reach this stage.

7.2.7 Other possible, and less common, outcomes

There are two further outcomes which may be allowed for in your university's regulations, but which are extremely rare. The first of these is the situation where the examiners feel that the candidate's thesis is at the right standard, but the performance in the viva is not adequate. In such circumstances, it is usually possible to refer the candidate in the viva alone; that is, the candidate is required to have a further viva, even though the thesis is acceptable. Such an outcome is unlikely. If the candidate is able to produce a thesis of the right standard, the chances are that they will be able to defend their work adequately during a viva. I have never seen this situation happen; but it is possible, highlighting that the viva is an important and vital part of the assessment process, and distinct from the examination of the thesis.

The other possibility, that I have not yet discussed, occurs when the examiners feel that the thesis is so below-standard that there is no useful purpose in holding a viva at this stage. In such cases, the examiners may recommend that the thesis is sent back to the candidate for further work and improvement, and re-submitted at a later stage, at which point a viva will take place. Some universities' regulations do not allow this option because they feel that the viva is so integral to the assessment process that it must always take place. Another view is that the candidate should always have the right to defend their work, no matter how poor the examiners may feel it is. The situation which I have described here is rare, but it does happen.

7.3 The questions that the examiners have to consider

In this section I will cover the questions which the examiners have to answer at the end of the examination. These are included in the official documentation for the award of the degree and may include:

The thesis:

- Does the thesis represent a significant contribution to knowledge of the subject by the discovery of new facts and/or the exercise of independent critical powers?
- Does the thesis provide evidence of originality?
- Is the thesis satisfactory as regards literary presentation and succinctness?
- Is the abstract of the thesis submitted acceptable?

The viva:

- Are you satisfied that the thesis presented is the candidate's own work?
- Did the candidate show a satisfactory knowledge and understanding of matters relating to the thesis?
- Did the candidate show a satisfactory knowledge and understanding of background studies to the subject of the thesis?

The above questions are taken from the recommendation form of a UK university. Notice that a distinction is made between the two parts of the examination: the assessment of the thesis and the viva. Notice also that the concepts of contribution to knowledge and originality are specifically referred to, as is the need for satisfactory literary presentation and succinctness. Many theses are referred back to the student because of typographical and presentational errors, that is, because the thesis is not 'satisfactory as regards literary presentation and succinctness'! It is worth spending the additional time needed to ensure that your own thesis meets this standard.

The abstract is also singled out as an important element of the assessment, and I covered this in Chapter 5.

In terms of the viva, the test of authenticity is highlighted; as is the need to understand not only the literature on which your own thesis is based, but also the literature which surrounds your work.

> "Overriding feedback was positive with a request to make the abstract more succinct and reduce the complexity around the methodology chapter to express more clearly what was done."

7.4 After it's all over, and recovery

Once your thesis is finally approved by the examiners you will be required to produce the final bound version(s) for the university library (see Figure 7.2 for an image of a final bound thesis). The University will give you precise instructions to help you produce this. I always think the final, formal, bound thesis looks great, and something that the PhD graduate should be really proud of.

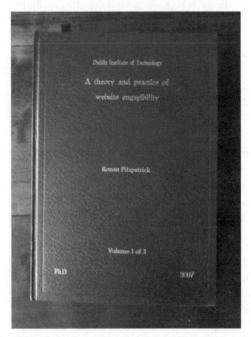

Figure 7.2   A final bound thesis ready to be lodged in the university library

Many thanks to Dr Ronan Fitzpatrick for allowing me to include this photograph of your thesis. I supervised Ronan for his PhD, which he undertook as a part-time student while lecturing at Dublin Institute of Technology. I spent many hours discussing his work during very pleasant visits to Dublin!

"The time went very quickly until I was waiting for the result of their deliberations ... the longest hour of my life! They were particularly keen to see consistency in the use of terms. I had deliberately tried to vary the words that I used to describe things (in relation to survey analysis) in order to reduce repetitiveness, however this had had the side effect of not making it clear that I was comparing 'eggs with eggs'. I was also amazed at how finicky some of the comments were (for example ensuring that the titles of tables were above rather than below). Overall it was clear that they were more than happy with my contribution, and less satisfied about the rigour of some of my writing."

You may feel somewhat deflated after your viva, whatever the outcome. Many of the students I have talked to expressed a feeling of anti-climax; almost of not knowing what to do with themselves after they'd had their viva. This is perfectly natural. You have spent three or more years of your life preparing for that day, and when it is finally over, you will undoubtedly be left wondering what your next steps are.

So take things easy after you have had your viva, and then, perhaps after a few days begin to plan your next steps, whether it be applying for jobs, or writing that paper that I have referred to at various points in the book.

And don't forget to attend the graduation ceremony. I always encourage my students to attend their PhD graduation ceremony. It is a very special occasion during which we can all celebrate the graduate's success, and think about all of the many years of hard work that went into that doctorate. It is also an important opportunity for you to thank your supervisors and other academic staff who have supported you throughout your PhD studies.

7.5 Appeals

If you have been awarded a lower degree than that for which you were registered, or if you have failed without the option of re-submitting, the only option left open to you may be the possibility of lodging an appeal. If you have reached this stage, you must first discuss things with your supervisor, and obtain a copy of the relevant regulations from your university. You must also check the time period for lodging an appeal, as it is likely that you will have to do so within a certain timeframe of the final decision being made by the university research degrees committee.

Your own university will have its own regulations and grounds on which a possible appeal can be lodged. These might include the following reasons:

- there were procedural irregularities in the conduct of the examination;
- there was some administrative error within the process of assessment;
- there is evidence of prejudice or bias on the part of one or more of the examiners;

- there is evidence of inadequate assessment by one or more of the examiners;
- there are personal circumstances which affected the candidate's performance of which the examiners were not aware when their decision was taken.

It may also be possible to raise issues with the supervision process if you feel that inadequate supervision has affected your performance. However, in many universities you would be expected to use the complaints procedure, rather than an appeals procedure, for issues relating to supervision, and the question may be raised as to why you did not complain about your supervision at an earlier stage of your PhD. You will not be allowed to question the academic judgement of the examiners.

An appeals process will normally have the following stages:

- An appeals panel will meet to decide if there is a case for appeal.
- If there is a case the appeal will be heard by a designated panel.

If your appeal is upheld the possible outcomes are likely to be:

- Your case will be passed back to the examination panel, who will be asked to reconsider their decision.
- The examination may be declared null and void and a further examination will be held, which may involve the appointment of a new examination panel.

As stated earlier, you must consult the regulations of your own university if you are in this situation. You must also take advice from your supervisor if you feel able to do so. The university students' union will also have a representative who will be able to advise you.

Summary

This chapter has discussed the possible outcomes which may arise from the PhD examination process. In each case, the implications and a way forward have been discussed. I hope this has given you an insight into all of the possible things that could arise as the result of a PhD viva. The next chapter includes a series of case studies of actual student viva experiences.

8 Case Studies

On completion of this chapter you will:

▶ have read the views of a number of students who describe their own PhD viva experiences
▶ understand a little of the 'lived experience' of a group of PhD candidates from a range of disciplines
▶ realise that the viva is something that you can be successful at, and not something to be feared
▶ be able to use the lessons from the student narratives to inform your own viva preparations

8.1 Chapter overview

This chapter presents a series of ten case studies of students and their viva experiences. These have been drawn from real students with whom I have had personal involvement, as their supervisor, examiner or the Chair of their examination. In all cases the students have agreed to their narrative accounts being included. The case studies first present a brief background to the student. The candidate then relates, in their own words, how they prepared for the viva, how the viva experience was for them, the nature of the questions that they were asked, the questioning process and the outcome. Where there was a need for revisions to the thesis, these are also discussed.

These case studies are then analysed and a series of lessons are drawn from them. The case studies cover a range of disciplines and a range of outcomes. The outcomes include: a pass at first attempt (with no changes, which is relatively rare), a pass with minor amendments, and a pass with major amendments. There is also one case study which includes a re-submission in which the candidate has to undertake further work, a second viva, and then ultimately passed. In all cases the narrative accounts show the lessons that the candidate has learned from the experience, and make some suggestions that you might use in your own viva preparations.

The students' names, and some other aspects of the case studies, have been changed in order to protect the anonymity of the candidates, the examiners and the students' supervisors.

I hope that these case studies will give you a deeper understanding of the entire viva process, and that you will be able to use them to inform your own viva preparations. As you read these case studies, I am sure that you will find that some will interest you more than others, dependent perhaps upon the subject area. However, there are some common themes running through these case studies which I draw together at the close of the chapter.

8.2 The case studies

These case studies present viva experiences in the student's own words. Each case study covers the following areas:

- Background: A brief introduction to the student and their PhD subject area
- Preparations prior to the viva
- Mock viva
- The night before, and the morning, of the viva
- The viva itself
- The outcome
- After the viva
- Advice for other students
- Summary and final points

The student's own words appear in italics throughout this chapter. I have reproduced the students' words exactly as they were given to me (other than a small amount of rewording in some cases to help with readability or to protect anonymity). Some of the students have made comments that I don't agree with, and I did think about removing some of them. In the end, however, I felt it better and more authentic to leave the narratives as they were given to me. You will find that there are a range of views here, and that they give you quite a few different interpretations to consider. Ultimately, however, you will need to form your own opinion as to the best way to prepare for *your* viva. It is a personal choice and I hope that you find these accounts useful in making that choice.

8.2.1 Case study 1: Tony

Background

Tony enrolled for his PhD after completing his undergraduate degree at the same university. His project was in media and cultural studies.

Preparations prior to the viva

My preparation consisted mainly of re-reading the thesis over and over again. Sometimes I'd take a few hours to go through the whole thing; sometimes I'd just do one chapter in a night. I didn't have pre-prepared answers as such, but I'd used a lot of sticky notes to highlight particular parts of the thesis, with each colour signifying a particular part of the argument that they might ask about – e.g., previous work I'm building on, evidence of textual analysis, evidence of originality, etc. My supervisors tried to guide me as best they could, but overall their best advice was to rely on what I knew – they kept stressing that no-one in that room knew my thesis better than me. They also told me not to be scared to answer 'Sorry, I'm not sure on that one' if a difficult question arose – the advice being that it's always better to be honest, than to try and bluff it out. I don't recall reading anything particularly useful beforehand.

Mock viva

I did not have a mock viva. I could have had one if I'd asked, but after advice from other students and staff I decided not to, which was a decision I always completely agreed with. If it had gone badly, I would have been much more nervous going into the real thing. If it had gone well, I could have been too relaxed or under-prepared for the real thing. And there is no guarantee that the exact same questions will be asked in the real and mock viva, and no guarantee that the same answer will be taken as satisfactory.

The night before, and the morning of, the viva

I did nothing on the evening, taking the view that if I didn't know the thesis well enough by then, I would never know it well enough. Instead, I tried to relax as much as possible, watching a film to take my mind off it and then having an early night. I was understandably nervous the day of the viva, but as it was in the morning, it was a case of getting straight into it, rather than letting the tension build throughout the day.

The viva itself

I actually enjoyed the viva much more than I anticipated. The atmosphere was friendly and respectful with a genuine sense of the examiners being interested in my work, rather than being interested in actually examining me; if that makes sense. There was certainly no sense of them trying to trip me up, as it were. In terms of questions and approach, it was essentially what I was expecting. Although I can't recall the opening question exactly I think it was asking where the specific idea for my thesis topic came from. The questions started off quite general in nature and then fell into a structure where they went through the thesis chapter-by-chapter. I think it lasted around an hour in total. To my best recollection it ended with them thanking me for my time and saying that they had enjoyed reading my thesis.

The outcome

I was asked to return to the examination room after about half an hour. I was told I had passed the viva, but needed to make substantial corrections to achieve the PhD. I was very pleased to have passed and, due to circumstances during the writing of the PhD, I was fully expecting to have major corrections to make. Generally, I was relieved and happy with this outcome.

After the viva

At first, I struggled to take in the fact that this was a major hurdle I'd overcome and would never have to do again. However, this was tempered with the knowledge that I had corrections and a lot of work still to do. The corrections were sent out in the post to me and quite detailed. Most were clear, although my supervisor was able to query, clarify and in a couple of cases, go back to the examiners and question some of them. I did need a lot of help with them, particularly the last sweep of them as my supervisor had left her position by then.

Advice for other students

I would advise students to seriously question whether they need a mock viva or not. I think it has more pitfalls than benefits. If you get nervous, I think you'll still get nervous for the real thing. I would also advise you to not have your supervisor present, as I was given the option of. This is because the temptation to look to them for advice for a difficult question (which they can't give) may be too great. Ultimately, you have to defend and explain your work yourself and being in there on your own is the best way to do that. It's also quite liberating as a lot of PhD work will be done from suggestions by supervisors – them not being present means you can state all the ideas were yours to begin with! That was an actual piece of serious advice given to me. There may be parts of the PhD that you've had strong disagreements with your supervisor over, and having that tension in the room is not a good idea.

I would also advise a student to remember that no-one knows your thesis as well as you do. Vivas aren't mean to be confrontational and the examiners are not setting out to trick you. The examiners will be asking questions that you will know the answers to. Take your time for each answer and sip water in-between; this gives you room and space for thought. You don't get any extra credit for giving a speedy answer. And certainly don't lie or bluff – if you don't know, it is much better to just say so. Make a list of relevant points and page references that you think support the argument of each chapter and have that to hand during your viva. Make sure you know what the point of each chapter is; what the concluding argument of each chapter is and how the next chapter develops it. Ultimately, you can be in control of your viva as much as the examiners – you can ask for questions to be repeated, take as much time as you need, take in pre-prepared sheets with reference points etc., and stress just why you think it is valid work you've done.

Summary and final points

Tony worked with his supervisor on the changes to his thesis. They took longer than he expected to complete, as the nature of them was quite substantial. The changes did not involve the collection of further data; rather they were about the analysis of his findings and how they were presented within the thesis.

Tony felt quite strongly that he would not have benefited from a mock viva, his reason being that he felt it cannot possibly adequately represent the real thing. He also felt that a mock viva had the potential of making him even more nervous about his actual viva. I have experienced a few other students who have expressed similar views and some of those were persuaded to have a mock viva. In all cases, they did find the mock viva to be very useful.

8.2.2 Case study 2: Sarah

Background

Sarah studied for her PhD part-time while holding down a full-time job in a local college of further education. Her PhD was in education.

Preparations prior to the viva

I re-read the thesis and prepared answers to questions just as I would for an interview for a job. I spoke to my supervisors about the questions and then revised the answers, taking account of their advice. I googled information about the viva in general and read a few books, one that a fellow student had given me. I read the university booklet on the PhD viva.

Mock viva

My final annual review took the form of a mock viva. I found it very useful; it reassured me that I was able to defend my work; although I was more comfortable with some aspects of my thesis and less comfortable with some others. This helped me to fill any necessary gaps during my viva preparations. I found the mock viva every reassuring as the panel was very supportive and this spurred me on to prepare well.

The night before, and the morning of, the viva

The night before my viva I re-read the questions and answers that I had prepared and rehearsed my description of the thesis in preparation for the first, opening, question that I anticipated. My viva was scheduled to take place during the afternoon. On the morning of the viva I had a normal day at work with a meeting with my boss, this was very good as it took my mind off my nerves. I felt prepared and almost excited about the viva.

The viva itself

I enjoyed it. There were some questions that I was expecting and they didn't ask, and others that I hadn't anticipated. I was surprised that the Chair only 'chaired' and left the talking (and questioning) to the examiners; I guess this seems obvious now, but I found quite strange on the day. It was shorter than

I thought it would be, I can't quite remember but I think it was less than an hour and a half; and then there seemed like a huge wait before we (my supervisor and I, that is) were brought back in.

The outcome

The Chair shook my hand and said 'Congratulations' but it is a bit of a blur. I was elated!

This was a rescheduled viva as the external examiner had been poorly and my first viva was postponed as a result (which was frustrating but unavoidable in the circumstances). I had also changed jobs so the work seemed to have taken place quite a long time ago. I think I talked about it well but I made a schoolgirl error of saying things that weren't as explicit as they should have been in the thesis and was then given quite a lot of small amendments to do.

[Note from the author: I was present at the viva, and I am sure that although Sarah may think this is the reason she had those amendments to make, I am also sure that this was not the case.]

After the viva

The corrections were very clear and involved some extra work but were a lot about the structure of the thesis which I agree is a lot clearer now. It was hard work but I got some good advice from my supervisors about just doing it and getting on with it; and this is what I did. I gave myself a month off and then gave myself a month to do the amendments – which I then sent to my supervisors for comments. My supervisors made some suggestions which I incorporated into the final thesis and I then submitted to the university. The examiners had agreed that it would be reviewed by the internal examiner only.

It felt like a very long wait but the internal examiner had a family emergency which meant that it is was about 7 weeks before I found out I had passed but I was delighted, and very relieved when I got the good news. I had a lovely day at graduation with my family and my supervisors, and am now planning to write a further paper based on my work.

Advice for other students

Approach it like an interview for a job you really want to get and prepare as such.

Enjoy it! I certainly did.

Do the amendments as quickly as you can and don't dwell on them

Publish something during your PhD studies. I published one paper during my studies and presented a poster at a conference. I felt that these activities prepared me well for the viva. I also felt that the examiners seemed impressed that I had already published some of my work, and that this helped me during the viva.

Summary and final points

Sarah enjoyed her viva, and found a mock viva helpful. She also published a journal paper during her studies, which impressed the examiners. Her amendments were largely structural. The examiners felt her work made a clear contribution, but they weren't convinced that the thesis presented that contribution in the best possible way. They asked her to reorder some of the material and to add some further discussion of her results. She did not have to do any further research work, or collect any more data. Her PhD has helped her to gain a new job, and she is currently working on a further journal paper.

8.2.3 Case study 3: Laura

Background

Laura was a full-time teacher and studied for a professional doctorate part-time. The topic of her professional doctorate was science education. Her submission took the form of a report and a portfolio of evidence, rather than a traditional thesis. She was examined by three examiners; two external examiners (one from a university and one from her own profession, and an internal examiner). The regulations of the professional doctorate programme on which she was studying require the examination panel to be constituted in this way.

Preparations prior to the viva

I prepared, in the preceding weeks, by reading my portfolio of eleven reports, as well as the overarching critical reflection report. I made notes, so that I could quote references and sources of information, as well as methodologies.

Several friends have PhDs, although all in scientific disciplines (astrophysics, particle physics, biology and chemistry). By all accounts, their vivas were rigorous and thorough processes, although related to specific experiments. They all warned me, however, to be prepared!

After the mock viva, I invested even more effort into preparation – it was all I could think about for the week before the actual viva. I thought that I had prepared fully, although after submitting in December, then having a mock viva in February and the actual viva in March, I had sufficiently reflected upon my work so that I could anticipate areas of questioning.

The guide sent to me by the university was particularly useful.

Mock viva

The mock viva was extremely useful, where I was 'challenged' by lecturers within the department. It was certainly not a comfortable chat about my work, as I was interrogated and challenged for about an hour and a half on all aspects of my work. Having said that, the experience was supportive and encouraging, and the feedback was really useful. I would recommend everyone to have a mock viva.

It was excellent preparation, although it did not reassure me, far from it! It highlighted areas that could be challenged by the external examiners, so the experience encouraged me to step up my preparation for the actual viva.

The night before, and the morning of, the viva

On the night before, I read through my notes and various aspects of my work. I was not unduly worried, as I expected that I would be challenged for a couple of hours, then given some corrections to do, then go back to work in the afternoon.

I knew there were some areas that could be criticised, but just expected this to be in the same way that the mock viva had been. I was looking forward to discussing my work with respected academics.

The viva itself

The three examiners were friendly and welcoming, with each having read my report in detail. Some of the questions were anticipated, exploring specific areas of my work in detail, but some questions went along completely different tracks to that which I expected. All of the questions were related to the critical reflection report, with none of the questions relating to the portfolio of reports submitted.

I remember the principal examiner kept pushing me to define what I meant by professional practice, and what texts I had read about 'practice'. He also questioned me in detail about the methodology behind my case studies. Although I had a chapter on methodology, he seemed to want even more detail.

During the viva, there were occasions where we all agreed on some topics and it turned into a pleasant conversation, but then in minutes it would turn to a different topic where I would feel under attack and having to defend particular decisions.

I can't remember how long the viva took – it seemed to go on for an endless eternity, although it must have been only about 2-3 hours.

Overall, I would say that the viva itself was fair, not too unpleasant but definitely thorough.

The outcome

After waiting for what seemed to be an eternity in the reception area, I was summoned back to the room. Although the examiners were very friendly, they told me that I needed to make some major corrections. These included a range of typography errors, references to approximately 15 other texts and papers and to further develop the theory behind the methodological approach I had taken.

As the feedback went on (it seemed to go on for ages!) I was convinced that I had failed. I took the feedback far more personally than I had anticipated. I was emotionally drained by the whole experience.

After the viva

There was the official list of corrections that came through the post, but each examiner had carefully inserted 'post it' notes into copies of my report, indicating where minor typing errors needed to be corrected.

Of the texts that were suggested to enhance my report, none were in the University Library. All needed to be obtained by inter-library loans, taking weeks and months to obtain (most were out of print). Two of the suggested texts had to be obtained from Trinity College, Dublin. Another two of the books that were strongly recommended were written in 1967 and 1972 – I read each of these rather old books several times, perplexed as I really could not see how they could help my report.

I must admit that I felt particularly frustrated at this point, as I believed that the examiners did not quite understand the point of a professional doctorate. I had compiled a portfolio of eleven sections, which totalled 83,000 words and my overarching critical reflection report was 42,000 words. One of the criticisms that I expected at the viva was to be told off for exceeding the suggested word count!

After making all of the corrections from the viva, my overarching report then totalled 60,000 words. All of my friends with PhDs were quite astonished at the amount of work required for a professional doctorate, particularly compared with science doctorates.

I devoted every spare minute of every day to completing the corrections, taking about 4 months instead of the suggested 6 months. My supervisors were excellent throughout, providing support, encouragement and advice to get me through. I felt that the corrected report was a better, much stronger version than the one that I had originally submitted, and was quite proud of my work. When the final email said that I had completed everything, the only emotion that I recall is relief!

Whilst my managers at work were neither interested nor supportive of my studies, I enjoyed the licence it provided to ask for information and question decisions.

Advice for other students

I expected questions about the work in the portfolio, but that was not touched upon.

Unlike science PhDs, the professional doctorate is a much more personal experience, a synthesis of your personal as well as professional values.

I would advise students to be prepared not just for the questions, but for the criticisms, which can seem harsh when one individual faces a panel of three or more people.

Summary and final points

Laura performed well during her viva, but her examiners felt that the methodological aspects of her work required underpinning with further theory and some additional reference to seminal literature. She had to read some further papers and texts and incorporate those into her submission. After doing so, everyone (Laura herself, her supervisors and the examiners) all felt that her submission was much improved.

8.2.4 Case study 4: Sally

Background

Sally was undertaking a professional doctorate in a sociological topic. She was working full-time at the same time as studying for her doctorate. Her submission took the form of a report and a portfolio of evidence, rather than a traditional thesis.

Preparations prior to the viva

As the date for the viva drew close I had made a conscious effort to block out time each night after work, and this was very much like the time I had previously allocated to writing up, editing and the re-editing process. I went back to a hard backed book that I had kept from my very first tutorial sessions, and the proposal stage of the research. I became very much aware that the essence of my subject remained the same, but there was a greater simplicity and pithiness to the final version of design and questions in contrast to my former supposed sophistication. For this, I must firstly acknowledge and secondly thank my supervisors for their greater wisdom.

I had read and used all the activities in a book provided for all students by the programme leader. The book was 'Achieving your Professional Doctorate' by Nancy Jane Lee (2009). I went back to what I had written, and considered why some of the tasks had been to draw out my report design in diagrammatic form. When re-visiting a visual overview of my early planned study this proved to be helpful as it illustrated many of the composite parts, which made up the whole doctoral report. As a process, it helped me realise the changes to my thinking and learning. This personal critique, in a personal mode, and personal space helped me to deconstruct some former poor ideas and reconstruct and recognise where and when my supervisors had projected me forward toward new forms of knowledge.

This was only the tip of the iceberg! I spent the six weeks before the viva reading and re-reading Trafford and Leshem's book (2008), and their paper

(2002b) that include 'predictable questions', conceptual ideas, and the due processes of the viva. I also got fairly creative and drew out new diagrams of each section of my study, and considered at length the purpose of my writing and stylistics.

Mock viva

I did have a mock viva and I was given mixed messages from peers and staff as to how useful/or not this would be. However, it was my choice to experience a mock viva as this was beyond my know-how, and I wanted the experience. On the day in question, I felt the room and the positioning of chairs was a little uncomfortable and not a true reflection of the possible event. It seemed to be a 'pretend' situation rather than a pilot run of the real viva.

The staff who questioned me about my study were openly friendly, and bordering on being familiar; which was not surprising since I knew them well. But this was a little off-putting; I wanted more formality, so that it would more closely model the real situation. There was one member of staff who remained cool, and professionally distant. It is from this person that I learned the most. At the close of the mock viva I was offered back an annotated copy of my report, and I received germane comments about my work and ideas on how to verbally present responses on the actual day of the viva; this remained in my head.

The night before, and the morning of, the viva

I had prepared an A4 file full of diagrams and imagery on each one of the chapters, this was for me to wholly know and understand each element of the doctoral report. Additionally, I had completed the questions posed by Trafford and Leshem. The questions I had answered in full and in my own handwriting, additionally, I had carried out a critique of my writing in terms of style and genre for each chapter. The file was in chapter order and I could dip in and out of it, this really helped me to understand the structure and format of the doctoral report (wished I had known about this earlier) as well as the complementary nature of the portfolio that was cross referenced in the report and provided evidence of doctoral work and publications.

On the day of the viva I was calm, and I felt refreshed, I ate a small breakfast, set out in comfortable clothes and in plenty of time, because I did not want to encounter traffic or parking problems.

I made an effort to bracket any negativity, and tried not to internalise the 'horror' stories and negative things I had been told about others' encounters and viva. I only allowed a couple of minutes with my supervisor before entering the viva as I did not want to lose my concentration and composure. The Programme Leader was there to wish me luck; this I thought was a 'human touch', particularly kind and thoughtful given their role and responsibilities.

The viva itself

From the moment I entered the room I was put at ease, and informed that the viva was to be an academic discussion. I was told not to worry unduly given that my work had something very interesting to convey and that it was at the expected doctoral level.

I loved the discussion, I really, really did! I was asked six questions and these were in my specialist subject area, it was at this point and for the first time I truly realised this. The notion of being a specialist with a unique voice was explicitly reinforced by one of the examiners whose comments included that I 'was a specialist in the field' and that I 'needed to walk out of the viva knowing I should be recognised as such'. The questions asked were indirectly related to what I had prepared – a series of hybrid questions. The panel seemed genuinely or more interested in my story, in particular, how I had begun, reflections on my ability to engage and influence others, and how I reached the endpoint.

The process of questioning lasted just under one hour; the whole viva was over within one hour and twenty minutes. Comments made by the examiners suggested it was the shortest viva that they had ever taken part in. I recall at one stage an examiner leaned back on his chair and rubbed the top of his head, and then he laughed out loud at my use of an established theoretical model in a new way. I observed his behaviour; he leaned toward me, this most distinguished author in the field, and conveyed genuine warmth of feeling across the table. He was hooked into my study and he was emotionally engaged in discussion of my learning, and about the sharing of 'new knowledge'.

There was no page by page sequence of questioning rather engagement with me about my learning journey and my doctoral study and my process of learning.

The outcome

I was congratulated within an hour and five minutes and when it was time to leave I was told to walk out of the room as 'Dr...' There were some minor tasks to consider, but the outcome of the viva however was clear.

I had made such a conscious effort to bracket any negativity when the viva was over it seemed as though it was a bit of a non-event or anti-climax, rather than an outright success. I recall thinking that I had paid for four hours' parking in the university car park and yet I hadn't even used up two hours. I sat for a few minutes with my supervisor in a sort of haze and remember telling her that I would have liked to have telephoned my Mum to tell her the news, but she died five months earlier. The next contact on the list was my husband who was elated and insisted we were celebrating by going out for dinner.

After the viva

As mentioned above, in the immediacy of the moment it is important to remember to be polite and so forth, but when you get back into the stillness and quiet of your own home and or working role (and mine is in academia) the responses from those around can be somewhat surprising and or polarised.

But with an attitude of 'that's it', 'it's over', and 'you've got it' my own adult children were glad to have their Mum back.

The corrections were small and set out clearly for me to address and included typos, minor referencing and a short addition to a reflective element, therefore I liaised with my supervisor but did not feel that I required their help at this stage. I do believe that supervisors play a pivotal role in enabling students to retain a sense of equilibrium and suggest this perhaps is under reported.

When the degree was confirmed it was just another piece of paper that dropped on the door mat, it had little significance unlike the energy and impact of lively discussion during the viva. The viva and confirmation of degree separated me from my peers and critical friends on the doctoral journey. There were some who were either ahead of me, taking time out, or behind me in terms of finishing; there was a sense of being uncoupled or disconnected rather than belonging to a community of learners and learning.

Advice for other students

The single and most important piece of advice I would give is to plan for this part of the doctoral journey, just like each other stage. Also do allocate time to read and write up what you want to say during the viva. If like me, you are a creative learner use the diagrammatic form to capture the essence of your chapters, and truly and honestly understand the genre, style and structure of your own writing. I took great heart from Rugg and Petre (2007) who had included in their book the notion of don't get it right, get it written.

As you get to the close of your study, if your story or doctoral report is ready you will recognise this. Remember that your situation is unique to you; avoid those who criticise, especially those unwilling to proffer critical advice. Smile, show a sense of tenacity – humour is good too, accept with good grace any compliments given to you and your work (don't down play this). When moments of doubt creep in keep your own counsel and try not drink copious amounts of fizz, or red wine!

Summary and final points

Sally greatly enjoyed her viva. Her examiners were particularly impressed by her work, and the viva became an interesting and stimulating discussion for all of them. She found the mock viva useful, but would have preferred it to be more formal so that it more closely resembled the real thing. She had put a lot of time into preparing for her viva, including reading about the viva process, and planning some questions that might be asked. She also summarised her submission, choosing to do so pictorially, rather than using words. Her doctorate helped her to move to a new position with a new employer.

8.2.5   Case study 5: Roy

Background

Roy was a part-time PhD student in urban design. He spent more than 5 years completing his studies. Roy is a retired town architect /planner, who is working as a private consultant. He is also lecturing in urban design to Master's students at a local university.

Preparations prior to the viva

About three weeks prior to the viva I consulted both supervisors, other academics familiar with my work and practitioners about likely questions, methodology, structure, the arguments I should put forward etc. I read through my thesis twice, and very thoroughly. I researched the background of my examiners, googling their CVs and reading some of their publications to try and get a feel for the type of questions which they might ask me. Prior to being given a date for my viva, I started a 'running list' of possible questions, which I added to whenever a new possibility entered my head. This proved to be invaluable in preparing me for the real event.

Mock viva

I had a mock viva well in advance of the real viva. In fact it was some months in advance, given the time it took for my real viva to be scheduled. The mock viva took place as I was finishing writing my thesis, and forced me to 'freeze' the work, i.e. to stop making any further changes or amendments to my thesis. Having the thesis printed and seeing the final product (It looked great J) was a big stimulus.

The mock viva was with a relatively recent PhD graduate and a senior academic: two people that I knew beforehand. This made the mock seem a little too informal, and in retrospect, lacking in real rigour (unlike the real viva which was very searching). However, the mock viva feedback gave me confidence that the work was readable and well presented.

The night before, and the morning of, the viva

The day before the viva I was still preparing and re-reading my list of possible questions. The evening before – was a normal evening!

On the day of the viva (which was at lunchtime) I deliberately did not do any further preparation, spending time assembling my brief case of items which I could use in support of my thesis and, above all, getting organised and ready to look professional, well prepared and confident.

The viva itself

The viva was scheduled to start at 1.30pm. It started at 1.40pm and finished at 3.25pm. Prior to the viva I met my external examiner in the corridor. He introduced himself (he recognised me from photographs in my thesis). This was a great 'ice breaker'.

The questioning seemed intense and the examiners were very well prepared (one of them had a very long typed list of issues!). They had obviously thoroughly read my thesis! The process was not done by order of chapters, but covered issues with each examiner asking questions in turn. Many of the questions were ones which I had <u>not</u> anticipated on my list! The viva was very searching, quite intense, and certainly no 'push over'.

The outcome

After nearly two hours I was asked to leave the examination room being told that the chairperson would retrieve me for the examination panel to tell me the outcome. This interval was less than five minutes.

On re-entry to the examination room I was extremely nervous. The internal examiner was asked to tell me the outcome which was delivered thus: 'Congratulations, Roy, you can call yourself Dr Stevens'. My reaction was 'That's fantastic – but what about the amendments?' I was then told that the examiners did not require any amendments. This was <u>exhilarating</u> news. The examiners and I then had an informal discussion for several minutes – a very nice ending to a rewarding afternoon.

After the viva

The viva took place in mid-November and the Graduate School notified me formally a few weeks later and indicating that the examiners' decision needed to be presented to an academic committee in February. After the viva I was so exhausted that I did not organise the final reprinting and binding (for the library copies) until the following April. This was six years from enrolling on the part-time PhD programme! I was very ambivalent about attending the graduation ceremony, although I did so, and enjoyed the day.

Advice for other students

Start a list of possible questions well before the viva. Continue to add to this as your viva approaches. You will find that you include many questions which will never be asked during your viva, but it is better to be prepared.

Research the background of your examiners, so that you have some idea of the type of things that they may ask you.

See your supervisors and others who have attended your annual review meetings for guidance, advice, support, etc.

Thoroughly read and re-read your thesis so that you know where to find something quickly in the viva if necessary.

For the viva itself – look professional, organised and knowledgeable.

Don't be arrogant in the viva, and don't 'take on' the examiners. There are ways of conveying that you have a different view point to the examiners. Engage in discussion with them, but don't argue with them.

Project your knowledge and experience of your subject.

Summary and final points

Roy did an excellent and very thorough job in preparing for the viva. He spent a long time revising his thesis, and this showed. The examiners were completely satisfied with his thesis; this is one of the rare occasions where the thesis was accepted 'as is' without any revisions at all: clear passes do happen!

Roy made a similar point to Sally; he felt his mock viva should have been more formal.

8.2.6   Case study 6: Maria

Background

Maria was a part-time PhD student in education. She was working full-time while studying for her PhD, and changed jobs and employers during her studies.

Preparations prior to the viva

My preparation included reading and re-reading my thesis and trying to see it through 'new eyes'; that is the eyes of the examiners and trying to imagine what I would ask if I was them. I did prepare answers to standard questions and some these were helpful to me on the day; for example: how is this a unique contribution to knowledge? etc. My supervisors advised that I became an expert in my methodology, and my subject, what had been written in the past, its appeal and appropriateness and its detractors. This is excellent advice. As much as anything it helps with confidence on the day.

Mock viva

The mock viva was with people that I had never met before. It was helpful in that it helped focus my thinking and it was additional preparation. I prepared as if it was the real event. However I didn't feel that it was really very rigorous (the mock examiners weren't specialists in my field) and certainly in my case it wasn't anything like the real thing.

The night before, and the morning of, the viva

I didn't do anything except try to relax and get a good night's sleep.

The viva itself

In many ways the viva was what I expected in terms of the questions but it was made disconcerting from the beginning by being made to wait what seemed like an inordinate amount of time whilst the examiners had their pre-meeting. I was really well-prepared and I felt that I answered the questions confidently and cogently. Only one examiner behaved the way I expected. As the viva progressed I began to feel that two of my three examiners had different views of my work and they were moving farther apart as the viva progressed. At times I felt like a chew toy between two dogs and at one or two points in the viva it appeared to me that neither one would give way to the other. I felt almost secondary to their differences, their silent argument.

When I came out my supervisor thought I had done really well and expected a very positive outcome. However, I had a nagging doubt. As we waited for the result, which seemed to take for ages, it confirmed to me again that there was some kind of tussle. So I was left at the end with a feeling that the outcome (major corrections) was in some way unjustified. In the end I realised that it wasn't – my thesis ended up being so much better after some re-writes – but the feeling that it was unfair and not just a honest reflection on my thesis could have destroyed me. It was only the support of my supervisors and my determination to pass that helped me to pick it up again. The temptation to give up is great, almost overwhelming. However, the motivation that started it all in the first place – being able to be called doctor, and actually finishing a major piece of work that I had started, was greater. So I had a (short) rest, a break from it, and got back on track. I think what got me through this was a fundamental belief that I had something worthwhile to contribute.

The outcome

See above. [Note: Maria was asked to do some further work, including work on the theoretical underpinning of her thesis, and the collection of further data. She also had to undergo a further viva.]

After the viva

After the second viva, which I passed with only the most minor of changes I felt euphoric. It was over and I could sleep/breathe/relax. It seems like such a long time from starting to the final hurdle. Having the degree confirmed is simply the best feeling in the world. When I got in the car to drive home I burst into tears, then texted all my family and friends. Being able to call myself doctor is superb. I changed my title on everything – bank, credit cards etc.

Advice for other students

Don't listen to the horror stories/fairy tales about vivas. Some people seem to sail through it (not helpful when you don't) and some people suffer. Your's won't be like anybody else's.

Be prepared to defend your research. Remember that nobody is more of an expert on your thesis than you are. Know your methodology, its strengths and weaknesses, and why you chose that over others. You feel like they will ask lots of difficult questions – but remember that you are also an expert on the subject. Be confident and not hesitant in your answers. If you don't believe in your work, you won't convince anybody else.

But you are so close to your thesis, that it can become like a much loved child and you take all criticism of it personally. Avoid this or you won't move on.

Summary and final points

Maria's examiners felt that she needed to do some further theoretical work and collect some further data. They felt this was needed to support her contribution to knowledge. Although Maria and her supervisors were all disappointed at the outcome, she soon set about doing the work, arranged further interviews and collected the additional data. When she submitted the revised thesis, she realised herself that it was much stronger.

The examiners were very pleased with the additional work that she had done and, as a result, her second viva was relatively short. It became a pleasant discussion of her thesis and how she felt the additional work had strengthened her contribution.

Interestingly Maria made a similar point to some of the other case study students; she felt her mock viva could have been more formal.

8.2.7   Case study 7: Amal

Background

Amal studied for her PhD in business management as a distance student. She was studying at the same time as running her own business. Her supervision team changed during the course of her studies, as a result of members of staff leaving the university.

Preparations prior to the viva

Yes, I re-read my thesis, and searched through it for areas that might require further explanation. Where I found these I made notes and prepared answers to standard questions or those I felt might be asked. I discussed the viva with my supervisor who gave me some good advice as to the questions that might arise and how to best prepare for my viva. I researched the viva process to understand it better, to know what was required and to better prepare for the viva.

The mock viva

I was studying for my PhD as a distance student and although I was offered a mock viva it didn't seem practical to have one. But I wish I had done one; in hindsight I think it would have been useful. I am sure that one could have been arranged. Even a practice with my supervisors, perhaps using Skype, would have been useful.

The night before, and the morning of, the viva

The evening before I went through the thesis briefly and went to sleep early. I felt quite anxious on the day of the viva.

The viva itself

I felt that my viva was very thorough and actually I found it quite gruelling. In the first half of the viva I was quite enjoying the discussion, although overall it was much harder than I had expected it to be. They started with an opening question of: 'What motivated you to undertake this research?' which I think I answered quite well.

The examiners were systematic in their approach; moving from Chapter 1 through to Chapter 7 (my final chapter); asking specific and general questions as they worked their way through the thesis. They did not go page by page... they focused a lot on Chapters 3, 5, 6 and 7. Some of the questions were expected but several were not. The viva lasted close to 3 hours in total. It closed in agreement and cordially, but it was clear to me that there were some areas of my thesis which the examiners felt needed to be revised.

The outcome

The examiners told me the outcome (that I had passed subject to some revisions to my thesis), but I waited some time to get the full list of amendments which was sent to by email. I felt disappointed at the outcome, but overall I was pleased that I had passed the viva, although I still had some work to do to my thesis.

After the viva

After the viva I was relieved that I passed but disappointed that the external examiner did not agree with the model that I had based my work on, and asked me to reframe it using a different one. The list of corrections was sent to me by email, and it was very clear and specific. The corrections required a small amount of additional data collection. In effect I had to rewrite my methodology and literature review section. I did all the corrections with the help and support of my supervisors. The revised thesis was sent to both the internal and the external examiner for approval. After a short wait, I was told that I had passed and that I have been awarded my PhD degree, which is a massive relief to me; I am delighted!

Advice for other students

Do not take anything for granted... you may be asked anything.

I wish I'd had a mock viva in order to better prepare for the actual viva. However, I was studying at a distance and a mock viva didn't seem practicable at the time; although in hindsight I could probably have done something by Skype with my supervisors.

Choose your examiner wisely... it makes all the difference!!!

Summary and final points

Amal passed but had quite a lot of amendments to make to her thesis. In particular, the external examiner had some issues with the theoretical model on which she had based her work, and asked her to make some changes to the model. Although Amal did not see the need for the changes (and still doesn't!) she made the necessary changes and was awarded her PhD.

8.2.8   Case study 8: Diane

Background

Diane had undertaken a PhD by previous published or creative work. This enabled her to base her thesis on her 20 years of making creative glass work. This was a practice-based PhD, and the first part of her viva took the form of an exhibition of a selection of her glass work. Diane guided the examiners around the exhibition area, and discussed her work with them, answering their questions as they visited each piece.

Preparations prior to the viva

My PhD was by Existing Published or Creative Works in the field of art and design. It consisted of a commentary (thesis) about my own practice over 20 years, therefore I felt pretty confident about talking about the work. However I did re-read the thesis on more than several occasions.

Mock viva

My supervisor (a colleague in my department at the university) casually asked if I felt like I needed a mock viva, leaving me to choose. I decided I would have one and I asked another colleague who had sat through many vivas if he would go through some of the questions he knew to come up frequently in a viva. I knew I had to brush up on my methodology section so swotted hard before the mock viva so I would be able to answer chapter and verse to any question pitched from any angle.

At the mock viva he asked me the straightforward question 'What makes this submission a PhD?' I was floored. I had never really put together an oral argument as to why this was a PhD although it was clear to be seen in the writing. I found the mock viva to be a very useful preparation exercise. Writing an argument is quite different from verbalising it and sometimes you need to practise!

The mock was a very useful exercise and gives one a good idea about the kind of things that might be asked. Knowing what might be coming in the real thing can only be a bonus and boost confidence.

The night before, and the morning of, the viva

I had prepared as much as I could do the week of the viva, my teaching and work load permitting. Re-reading sections, copying out relevant comments I wanted to make sure I made and practising my argument in my head constantly. My viva was on a Friday morning so I set time aside during the week to practise responses to questions raised at the mock. I did this out loud (alone) to gain confidence. Later on in the week I met another colleague for lunch; who fired questions at me as we ate.

The night before I ate fish ('brain food' my mother calls it) and went to bed early. I felt as prepared as I could be by the morning of the viva so went in feeling I'd done as much as I could.

The viva itself

My viva took place in a room adjacent to where I had an exhibition of my work which covered the 20 year period of my practice discussed in my thesis. This was an invaluable icebreaker for me as I was asked by the examiners to talk about the work which was there in front of us. The work gave me visual reminders of what I need to talk about and get across to the examiners. The exhibition was also next to a broken lift where the doors kept opening and closing which was somewhat of a distraction but I was able to hold my thread. This was mainly due to being well prepared I think.

The external examiners were not aggressive interrogators as I might have feared. I was able to answer all the questions and would have enjoyed the whole experience more if I had felt that I could relax. I was a little on my guard waiting for the question that might floor me as had happened in the mock. This was not the case. I actually felt that the examiners were very fair and both the external and the internal examiners seemed genuinely interested in what I had to say and in the thesis itself.

The whole viva took an hour and a half and closed as all the questions the examiners had prepared were answered. I had been expecting much more of a grilling and was quite surprised when it was over so comparatively soon.

The outcome

I was asked to leave the room so that the examiners could decide the outcome. My supervisor and I went for a coffee. It was only half an hour before I was asked to return to the room but it felt a lot longer! I was informed by *the Chair that I had passed and was told of the minor corrections I would be asked to make. There were few so felt there was no huge mountain to climb again before I would be awarded the title of Dr! I was hugely pleased and relieved and phoned my nearest and dearest to let them know that the last 18 months of my bad temper had not been in vain.*

After the viva

The high of passing and the celebrations directly after the viva made the writing of the thesis worthwhile. I felt relieved and rather pleased with myself. As I had relatively few corrections which were fairly straightforward I decided to do them immediately. I was able to complete them within a couple of weeks and submitted them to the internal examiner who passed them very quickly. All was completed within less than a month of the viva. I didn't seek any further assistance from my supervisor.

After letting people know I was almost a Dr then the anti-climax set in and not being able to use the title until graduation made me 'put the whole experience away' and get on with my job. As a practising artist working to commission I am used to working hard to deadlines, finishing pieces of public art. When my artworks are installed I have to let them go and I kind of did that with the PhD. I had worked hard, passed the test and then let it go. It all felt quite strange.

When the degree was finally confirmed I felt so proud and pleased. It was a fitting way to acknowledge all the hard work I had done on the thesis. It was no longer a commission I had put away but something quite different. My parents who are both in their 80's were able to attend, having attended my BA graduation 30 years previously! It was a proud moment for me and for them.

Advice for other students
- *'Question spot' with your supervisor*
- *Talk to people that have been through the process*
- *Attend the mock to build confidence*
- *Practise out loud*

Summary and final points

Diane passed with very small changes, and was clearly well prepared for her viva. She was nervous, but greatly enjoyed the discussion with the examiners. I am not quite sure why she felt that she couldn't use the title 'Dr' until after graduation; the norm would be to use it once the degree has been awarded by the university, which is usually well before the actual graduation ceremony!

8.2.9   Case study 9: Hamid

Background

Hamid studied for a part-time PhD in Computer Science, while working full-time. He was working in the Middle East, but chose to study his PhD in the same university department from which he had graduated several years previously. This meant that he was studying at a distance, visiting his supervisors when he came home. Most of his supervisory meetings were done by Skype and he used DropBox a lot during the preparation of his thesis drafts.

Preparations prior to the viva

After I had submitted the original thesis, I spent a few weeks checking it line by line looking for typographical errors, grammatical errors, incorrect labels/ fonts and anything else that didn't look right – there were plenty of mistakes. I highlighted each error in the hard copy with sticky page markers and corrected the errors in the soft copy. In the viva I took the original hard copy thesis with me complete with the identified errors and this helped me to demonstrate to the examiners that I had found and corrected all of the typos/ spelling mistakes etc.

My supervisors advised me to re-read the thesis and prepare answers to standard questions, so I re-read the thesis, several times, and prepared answers to standard questions, which I found on the internet, and a few suggested by my supervisors. It was difficult to find any real advice on preparing for the viva.

Mock viva

I did not have a mock viva, I wanted one but time and distance didn't allow it to happen.

The night before, and the morning of, the viva

The two days before the viva I prepared flash cards on the questions that I anticipated coming up in the viva and drilled myself in answering the questions.
The night before the viva, I tried to relax and not read anything.
I was extremely nervous on the day of the viva – in fact I was terrified.

The viva itself

I was very nervous prior to the viva, and was nervous when I entered the room. The viva Chair and the external examiner were very friendly and did their best to put me at ease. I was most worried about the internal examiner, as I had encountered him before, and knew he had a tendency to ask probing questions.

The examiners had a lot of questions, but thankfully they were all things that I could handle – very few of the questions that I had practised came up. The questions were very specific, and referred to sections in the thesis – there were few general questions. The questions weren't really what I had expected and I was quite happy with the questions that they asked.

I can't remember the opening question now.

The examiners were very good and were positive when framing their questions, which put me at ease – the whole process seemed to avoid any confrontation. In some ways the viva was as I had anticipated – other than the positive attitude of the examiners.

They went through the thesis and raised their concerns and issues section by section – mainly looking for clarification regarding why I had done certain things and looking for evidence that I had understood the research approach that I had used.

I can't really remember how long the viva lasted, it was somewhere in the region of 2 to 2 and a half hours.

By the end of the viva I found that I was actually enjoying myself and welcomed the opportunity to talk to someone about my research – they had to stop me talking for too long on a couple of occasions.

The viva closed with the examiners thanking me for answering their questions, and the Chair closed the session. I was asked to wait outside the room while the examiners discussed the viva.

The outcome

I waited for about 15 to 20 minutes and then was asked to re-join the Chair and examiners.

The external examiner took the lead and told me straight away that I had passed subject to a number of revisions. He then went on to explain the changes that they were requesting – however I did not absorb any of this at the time as I was so relieved by the decision.

I was then asked to join the examiners, and my supervisors for a bite to eat and a cup of tea – a nice touch, I don't think that this normally happens.

As I left the building I was thrilled that I had eventually completed my PhD, however I did not truly believe that I had passed until the changes had been confirmed by the internal examiner.

After the viva

After the viva I was very relieved. I had a number of corrections to make, to most of the chapters, and I had 6 months in which to make the changes.

I received an email about 4 weeks later from the GRS office with a list of the corrections that I had to make – I would have preferred to have received this information earlier, as I lost nearly a month of my completion time.

The corrections required were relatively clear and I felt that I knew what was required – I asked my supervisor for some clarification on a number of points and she provided me with the feedback to help me progress with the changes. After that I carried on with the work, firing off the occasional email to my supervisor if I needed any advice.

I was very happy when I was notified that the changes had been accepted and that I had passed.

I enjoyed the graduation, but afterwards I had a distinct feeling of being at a loose end and asked myself – 'well what do I do now'?

Advice for other students

I think that I approached and prepared for the viva as well as I could, give that I was not exactly sure what to expect. Re-read the thesis, look for any errors, prepare answers to anticipated questions. I feel that the supervisor should be able to offer some advice on the type of questions to expect – however this is only speculation and one will not know until you are in the viva with the examiners.

My supervisor was with me in the viva and I felt that the moral support that was provided helped me in my performance on the day – though this will only help if you have a good relationship with your supervisor.

Summary and final points

Hamid enjoyed his viva, and passed with some relatively small corrections to the thesis. These were done quite quickly and he was soon awarded his PhD.

8.2.10 Case study 10: John

Background

John studied for a PhD in Engineering as a part-time student. He changed jobs towards the end of his studies, and found writing the final thesis a big challenge as he faced the time pressures of his new job.

Preparations prior to the viva

Re-reading of the thesis was absolutely essential in building up confidence before the panel. It had been a long time since I'd written some parts of the thesis, and I felt I would need to know where content was in order to discuss my work at the viva. I realised that it would be impossible to prepare for every possible question, it would be far more likely that individual members of the panel would pick themes that they were interested in, and ask me open questions. I did however use a range of study skills to help me memorise facts, particularly my main reference sources. The methods used included making short-hand notes, and re-reading them, using a Dictaphone and narrating key points and facts and then playing them back through the car stereo on journeys, and writing 'questions and answers' on key facts.

I would stress that these were just key facts. It would be impossible, and unwise, to memorise the whole of a doctoral thesis. There is of course no need to memorise the whole thesis; being able to recall key sources whilst talking in detail about what was done and why it was done, helps with confidence and helps demonstrate academic rigour. A colleague who had sat on a panel one year before sent me a list of 'do's and don'ts' for the panel. These were useful, but I had also read that, just like every doctorate, every panel is different, and this is the case so there are no hard and fast rules. The best advice my supervisor gave me was that I should be seen to reflect on any apparent criticism that came along during the panel, rather than adopting a confrontational position. This is the key balance to be struck, to be seen to be both defending your own work and to be a reflective practitioner, open to the ideas of others.

Mock viva

I had two mock vivas. The first was set up as an alternative to an annual review that was due. This was conducted in a way that subsequently proved to be very like the real panel, in that I was firstly asked to give an overview of certain aspects of my work, and then panel members would ask specific questions about what I had said and what they had read in my report. This was a positive experience, even though it highlighted areas of my work that still needed improvement.

The second mock viva took place shortly before the real viva, but due to time constraints lacked some of the formalities and structure of an actual panel. It also consisted mainly of direct questions about what the two panel members perceived as the key weaknesses of my work. Although not intentional, this tended to develop into a confrontation; in fact my immediate reaction was that it had been something of a disaster. However, after the panel I was able to work through the written comments of the two panel members, and realise that I could have pursued a better line of argument, or pointed to evidence elsewhere in the thesis, and given a more reasoned defence of my work. So, although a very worrying experience, it did have a positive outcome. I knew, or recalled, where key evidence was, and experienced the down side of adopting too firm a defence of my work.

It could be argued that it had gone badly because the two panel members were unfamiliar with my work and had focused entirely, and rather negatively, on what they perceived as weaknesses. The reality is that, given human nature and the diverse membership of a real panel, there is always a chance that one or more members of the panel would adopt a similar approach. It is best to be prepared for such an eventuality, and be ready to take the reflective high ground, ensuring that panel members see that you are taking their comments seriously. In the real panel I did this by ensuring plenty of eye contact and by making short written notes on what panel members were asking.

The night before, and the morning of, the viva

Both the night before the viva, and the morning before my viva, I went through the written notes I had made on the key points from my work. I think this is a matter of personal choice. Some people might prefer some sort of displacement behaviour, watching television or listening to music, to ensure that they felt fresh for the panel. I have always liked to do last minute revision, otherwise I would worry I hadn't done enough.

Obviously there is so much depending on the viva there would be something wrong if you weren't nervous. I ate breakfast but didn't eat anything else until the evening (the panel was late afternoon). I felt very calm once I arrived at the university. I would go as far as to say I was looking forward to the viva, because for me it was the culmination of many years' work. I wanted to bring it to a conclusion.

You have to look at it objectively, there should be no-one more expert in the room about your doctorate than yourself. Yes, there will be people who are more expert in some specific aspects, and more aware of some related work. But since this is always going to be the case, the only real issue is how well you can present your case to support your work, and how professionally you can recognise any weaknesses about what you did.

The viva

The viva turned out very well. It was a professional and critical discussion, and in the main I was asked to talk about what I had done, before being asked any more direct questions. I think it would be impossible to anticipate the questions: a lot depends on the background of the examiners. For instance, one of the examiners had a very strong mathematical background, so perhaps quite naturally was most interested in the statistical analysis in my work. The viva lasted just over two hours, but the time seemed to pass very quickly. It drew to a close with 'just a few final questions'.

The outcome

At the end of the panel, my supervisor and I were asked to leave the room, and we returned about 20 minutes later. The result was that I had 'passed with corrections'. I was given verbal feedback of a very positive nature, whilst at the same time, the required corrections were discussed. My overwhelming feeling after the viva was one of relief, not because the viva had been a difficult experience, but because there had been so much depending on its outcome: six years' work in my case. It was one week later before I received the official written outcome of the examination.

After the viva

There was some sense of anti-climax after the viva, because after the initial euphoria comes the realisation that there is still work to be done. There were three specific corrections I had to make, but one of them seemed considerably larger than had been suggested at the viva. The corrections were reasonably clear, and I discussed them with my supervisor before proceeding.

Advice for other students

I would only say that, just as no two PhDs are the same, no two vivas will be the same. You need to be familiar with your own work and be able to quote some of your references. The members of the examination panel have been through a viva themselves, so I think most examination panel members are on your side. There is a fine line between defending your own work and antagonising members of the panel, and it is better to err on the side of not antagonising anyone!

Summary and final points

John clearly prepared well for his viva, which was a very positive experience. He, like several of the other candidates, makes some points about the mock viva. The changes to his thesis were relatively minor and he completed them within a matter of days. The degree was then awarded.

8.3 Common themes

Examination of the case studies reveals some common themes:

- It is normal to be nervous, but you can, and will, enjoy the experience! All of the students said that they were nervous prior to the viva, but they enjoyed the experience, although some found it more difficult than others.
- It is your work. Be proud of it, and speak about it with passion, commitment and authenticity. All of the students made the point that they (of course) full understood the detail of their work, and could answer the questions that were posed to them in the viva.
- It is important to prepare. Each candidate had their own way of preparing for their viva, and they all put substantial effort into those preparations, including practising answers to typical questions, re-reading their thesis and having a mock viva.
- Have a mock viva. It will be useful practice for the real thing, but you must treat it as a practice at answering questions, and not as a rehearsal for the actual viva. A mock viva cannot predict the actual questions. All of the candidates who had a mock viva found it useful. The more formal the mock viva, the better, so that it resembles in structure and

format the real thing. Those who take part in the mock viva should prepare for it and treat it seriously.

● They all passed! Some of the students passed with very small (or, in one case, no) revisions to the thesis. Others had more work to do. In (almost) every case, the candidate recognised why they had been asked to do the work, and felt that it resulted in an improved thesis.

● Several students felt a strange sense of 'not knowing what to do with themselves' after the viva. Be prepared for a feeling of anti-climax. However, you may feel more like the graduate who referred to it as 'getting my life back'.

Summary

This chapter has presented a series of ten case studies of the lived viva experiences of actual students. I hope that reading through them helps you with your own viva preparations. The next chapter summarises the issues and areas which have been covered in the book, and presents a checklist of the activities that you might do in preparation for your own viva.

9 Summary and the Future

> **On completion of this chapter you will:**
> ▶ have checked out the major points which relate to your viva, and ensure that you have preparations fully in place
> ▶ think about the next steps you will take after enjoying your viva, and graduating with your doctorate

9.1 Summary of the main points

This chapter briefly draws together all of the main points raised throughout the text, and summarises them as a checklist. It also gives some final reflections on my own experiences as a supervisor, an examiner and a PhD viva Chair. Finally, we encourage you, as a student, to reflect on your own doctoral experiences, and to continue to work at doctoral level after graduation. The chapter also addresses the question: 'What happens next?' and encourages you to view your doctoral study as one part of a lifelong learning journey.

> *"When you have formally received the final outcome from the research committee your work can be bound and submitted to the university library, but don't forget to give your supervisor a copy. Make sure that you go and enjoy your graduation ceremony because it is a public acknowledgement of the value of your accomplishments. Now it is all over and it is at this point that you get your life back".*

9.2 Checklist

In the checklist on the pages which follow I have grouped together the main points from each of the chapters, covering all of the things that I think you should include in your viva preparations.

CHECKLIST OF MAIN POINTS: 1	Have you covered these?
Positive thinking	
Think of all of the positive aspects of your PhD study	
Write down the three accomplishments of which you are most proud	
Write down a list of the types of people who will be interested in reading your thesis	
Your thesis	
Read and re-read your thesis to be sure that you know it thoroughly	
Mark up your thesis with sticky notes at the start of each chapter and important sections so that it is easy to find and refer to them during your viva	
Produce a chapter summary highlighting the areas of your thesis that are likely to be questioned	
The literature	
Keep reading so that you continue to be up to date with the literature	
Select the papers and texts which are most important and relevant to your thesis and re-read these	
Summarise the most important points from these papers and make notes on how they underpin and inform your thesis	

CHECKLIST OF MAIN POINTS: 2	
Questions	
Produce a list of possible questions, make this a running list and add to it whenever you think of a new question that might arise	
Practise answers to these questions	
Think of questions which are specific to *your* thesis, including possible questions for each chapter	
Mock viva	
Ask your supervisor to arrange a mock viva	
Ask fellow students to question you about your thesis	
Try to explain your thesis to family and friends who are not familiar with the subject area	
Your examiners	
If possible, discuss possible examiners with your supervisor	
Research the background of your examiners	
Read papers by your examiners so that you understand 'where they are coming from'	
Dissemination	
Plan a paper for publication with your supervisor(s)	
Produce a draft of the paper	
If you have time, submit the paper for publication prior to your viva	

CHECKLIST OF MAIN POINTS: 3	Have you covered these?
Contribution to knowledge	
Think carefully about your contribution to knowledge	
Write it down in a single paragraph	
Practise explaining your contribution in 5 to 10 minutes; try this out with fellow students, friends and family	
Background resources	
Read any material or guidelines about the viva which are provided by your university	
If available, watch a video of a viva	
Produce a plan covering all of the points in this checklist	
Presentation (if you need one for your viva)	
Plan your presentation with your supervisor	
Produce the slides well in advance (and not too many!)	
Rehearse, and time, your presentation	
Well-being	
Maintain a healthy life style	
Start your preparations well in advance	
Think positive; you can and will enjoy your viva, and if you have prepared well you have nothing to fear	

CHECKLIST OF MAIN POINTS: 4	Have you covered these?
The night before	
Eat healthily; no alcohol	
Have a quick check on the final preparations: where is the viva room? time? travel arrangements; is your marked-up thesis ready?	
Get a good night's sleep	
The day of the viva	
Dress smartly – tidy, professional; but no 'overkill'!	
Arrive in plenty of time	
Be confident. Enjoy it! Good luck!	
After the viva	
Accept the outcome, and start work on any revisions	
Do any revisions to the thesis as quickly as you are able	
Be thorough when you make the revisions; follow the requirements of the examiners precisely and to the letter	
Graduation	
Attend your graduation ceremony	
Write that paper from your thesis	
Enjoy your success; ensure you thank your supervisors and everyone who helped and supported you during your studies	

9.3 My personal reflections

I have had the privilege of working with more than 100 PhD and DProf students across a 30-year period. Each student has their own personal motivation for studying their PhD, and every PhD project is different. What is common is the enthusiasm and passion that the student has for their studies. Every student approaches the viva with a mix of nervousness and enthusiasm, but almost without exception they enjoy the experience. Some students have, of course, performed better than others, and each examiner I have encountered had their own style and approached the viva in their own way. However, again, almost without exception every student ultimately succeeded and graduated with their PhD, including students who had major revisions to make to their thesis.

I have met many examiners, and each one has their own individual approach to a PhD viva. Some of more interested in methodology, and others in the subject matter. Some see the PhD as a training programme in research, and others as a detailed and deep exploration of a subject area (it is, of course, both of these and more). A few examiners that I have encountered were obsessed about the writing style, grammar and presentational aspects. But the examiners all share one thing in common: the belief in doctoral standards and in the importance of the PhD as a means of training the researchers of the future. And they have all, without question, been fair, professional and respectful of the candidate.

I have attended many vivas. Some have been longer than others, and some candidates have excelled, while others have had to rely on the examiners to help draw out their contribution and the strengths of their thesis. Some have been joyous, celebratory experiences, while others have not gone so well and the disappointed candidate has been asked to do some more work. However, in all cases, the viva has been a learning experience for the candidate, the examiners and me. I have enjoyed them all, and hope to continue attending vivas in the future.

I have written this book in the hope that my own experiences and those of my students can help other candidates be better prepared for their own viva, and get the most out of it, so that it can be an enjoyable experience.

9.4 What happens next?

When you graduate you will, of course, have a feeling of great achievement. You have worked very hard, and deserve your PhD, and should feel very proud of yourself. However, this should not be the end of your journey.

In the words of one candidate:

"I can honestly say that, if my work resulted in a fail, whilst I would naturally be disappointed, I could walk away knowing that I have personally developed in a way that I never anticipated. Consequently, I am about to embark on a further, very challenging, project on and will begin with the hard task of deep diving into the theory knowing that this will produce the kind of outcomes that I can comfortably defend and be proud of."

You should consider continuing to publish your work along with your supervisors after you graduate. It is likely that you have produced a lot of material during the course of your doctorate, and some of this could probably be quite easily converted into papers which could be submitted to a journal. It might be possible to publish your work as a book chapter, or in some cases, as an entire book. Research shouldn't stop at graduation. In many ways, your journey has only just begun. Be prepared to continue your learning journey, and to pass on your experiences and advice to other students.

Summary

This chapter has presented a checklist which summarises the activities and tips covered in the book. I hope that you have enjoyed this book and that it has helped you in your preparations for your viva. I have enjoyed the experience of writing it, and of working with PhD students over the years.

Good luck with your viva; I hope you enjoy it, and that it goes well.

Peter Smith

Professor Peter Smith
peter.smith@sunderland.ac.uk

References

Baldacchino, G. (1994) 'Reflections on the status of a doctoral defence', *Journal of Graduate Education*, 1(3).

Brenner, M. (1985) 'Intensive interviewing' in M. Brenner (ed.) *Research Interview: Uses and approaches*, London: Academic Press.

British Journal of School Nursing (2013) 'Pilot project to reduce pre-exam stress', *British Journal of School Nursing*, 8(7), 60.

Burnham, P. (1994) 'Surviving the viva: unravelling the mystery of the PhD oral', *Journal of Graduate Education*, 1(1).

Carter, B. and Whittaker, K. (2009) 'Examining the British PhD viva: opening new doors or scarring for life?', *Contemporary Nurse*, 32(1–2), 169–178.

Carter, S. (2008) 'Examining the doctoral thesis: a discussion', *Innovations in Education & Teaching International*, 45(4), 365–374.

Condie, J. (2013) http://socphd.wordpress.com/2013/06/07/dont-mock-the-importance-of-a-having-a-practice-viva/.

Craswell, G. (2005) *Writing for Academic Success: A postgraduate guide*, London: Sage.

Day, M. (2009) 'Clearing the final hurdle: the PhD viva', *Sport & Exercise Psychology Review*, 5(2), 54.

Day, R. and Gastel, B. (2012) *How to Write and Publish a Scientific Paper*, 7th edn, Cambridge: Cambridge University Press.

Dinham, S. and C. Scott (2001) 'The experience of disseminating the results of doctoral research', *Journal for Further and Higher Education*, 25(1), 45–55.

Dunleavy, P. (2003) *Authoring a PhD: How to plan, draft, write and finish a doctoral thesis or dissertation*. Basingstoke: Palgrave Macmillan.

Fontana, A. and Frey, J. (1994) 'Interviewing: the art of science' in N. Denzin and Y. Lincoln (eds) *Handbook of Qualitative Research*, Thousand Oaks, CA: Sage.

Fulton J., Kuit J., Sanders G. and Smith P. (2013) *The Professional Doctorate*, Basingstoke: Palgrave Macmillan.

Grabbe, L.L. (2003) 'The trials of being a PhD external examiner', *Quality Assurance in Education*, 11(2), 128–133.

Hartley, J. and Fox, C. (2004) 'Assessing the mock viva: the experiences of British doctoral students', *Studies in Higher Education*, 29(6), 727–738.

Hartley, J. and Jory, S. (2000) 'Lifting the veil on the viva: the voice of experience', *Psychology Teaching Review*, 9(2), 79–90.

Higham, M. (1983) *Coping with Interviews*, London: New Opportunity Press.

Holbrook, A., Bourke, S., Fairbairn, H. and Lovat, T. (2007) 'Examiner comment on the literature review in Ph.D. theses', *Studies in Higher Education*, 32(3), 337–356.

Johnson, D. (2005) 'Assessment matters: some issues concerning the supervision and assessment of work-based doctorates', Innovations in Education and Teaching International, 42(1), 87–92.

Joyner, R.W. (2003) 'The selection of external examiners for research degrees', Quality Assurance in Education, 11(2), 123–127.

Juniper, B., Walsh, E., Richardson, A. and Morley, B. (2012) 'A new approach to evaluating the well-being of PhD research students', Assessment & Evaluation in Higher Education, 37(5), 563–576.

Kiley, M. and Mullins, G. (2004) 'Examining the examiners: how inexperienced examiners approach the assessment of research theses', International Journal of Educational Research, 41(2), 121–135.

Leather, S. (2013) 'Are PhD examiners really ogres?', simonleather.wordpress. com/2013/05/07/are-phd-examiners-really-ogres.

Lee, N.J. (2009) Achieving your Professional Doctorate. Maidenhead: Open University Press/McGraw-Hill Education.

Leonard, D., Metcalfe, J., Becker, R. and Evans, J. (2006) Review of Literature on the Impact of Working Context and Support on the Postgraduate Research Student Learning Experience, Higher Education Academy.

Morley, L., Leonard, D. and David, M. (2002) 'Variations in vivas: quality and equality in British PhD assessments', Studies in Higher Education, 27(3), 263–273.

Mullins, G. and Kiley, M. (2002) '"It's a PhD, not a Nobel Prize": how experienced examiners assess research theses", Studies in Higher Education, 27(4), 369–386.

Murray, R. (2003). 'Students' questions and their implications for the viva', Quality Assurance in Education, 11(2), 109–113.

Murray, R. (2009) Writing for Academic Journals, Maidenhead: Open University Press.

Murray, R. (2011) How to Write a Thesis. Buckingham: Open University Press.

Pearce, L. (2005) How to Examine a Thesis, Maidenhead: McGraw-Hill International.

QAA (Quality Assurance Agency for Higher Education) (2008) The Framework for Higher Education Qualifications in England, Wales and Northern Ireland, The Quality Assurance Agency for Higher Education.

QAA (Quality Assurance Agency for Higher Education) (2011) Doctoral Degree Qualifications, The Quality Assurance Agency for Higher Education.

QAA (Quality Assurance Agency for Higher Education) (2012) UK Quality Code for Higher Education – Chapter B11: Research degrees, The Quality Assurance Agency for Higher Education.

Rugg, G. and Petre, M. (2007) A Gentle Guide to Research Methods. Maidenhead: Open University Press/McGraw-Hill Education.

Schon, D. (1983) The Reflective Practitioner: How professionals think in action, New York: Basic Books.

Smith, P., Curtis, H., Sanders, G., Kuit, J. and Fulton, J. (2011) 'Student perceptions of the professional doctorate', Work Based Learning, 2(1).

Stubb, J., Pyhalto, K. and Lonka, K. (2011) 'Balancing between inspiration and exhaustion: PhD students' experienced socio-psychological well-being', *Studies in Continuing Education*, 33(1), 33–50.

Thompson, J., Smith, P. and Cooper, B. (2012) 'An autoethnographic study of the impact of reflection and doctoral study on practice', *Work Based Learning e-Journal International*, 2(2).

Tinkler, P. and Jackson, C. (2000) 'Examining the doctorate: institutional policy and the PhD examination process in Britain', *Studies in Higher Education*, 25(2), 167–180.

Tinkler, P. and Jackson, C. (2004) *The Doctoral Examination Process: A handbook for students, examiners and supervisors*, Maidenhead: McGraw-Hill International.

Tinkler, P. and Jackson, C. (2008) 'The viva' in G. Hall and J. Longman (eds) *The Postgraduate's Companion*, London: Sage.

Trafford, V. (2003) 'Questions in doctoral vivas: views from the inside', *Quality Assurance in Education*, 11(2), 114–122.

Trafford, V. and Leshem, S. (2002a) 'Anatomy of a doctoral viva', *Journal of Graduate Education*, 3(2), 33–40

Trafford, V. and Leshem, S. (2002b) 'Starting at the end to undertake doctoral research: predictable questions as stepping stones', *Higher Education Review*, 34(1), 31–49.

Trafford, V. and Leshem, S. (2008) *Stepping Stones to Achieving your Doctorate*. Maidenhead: McGraw-Hill/Open University Press.

Wallace, S. (2003) 'Figuratively speaking: six accounts of the PhD viva', *Quality Assurance in Education*, 11(2), 100–108.

Wallace, S. and Marsh, C. (2001) 'Trial by ordeal or the chummy game? Six case studies in the conduct of the British PhD viva examination', *Higher Education Review*, 34(1), 35–59.

Wellington, J. (2010) 'Supporting students' preparation for the viva: their preconceptions and implications for practice', *Teaching in Higher Education*, 15(1), 71–84.

Yin, R.K. (2009) *Case Study Research: Design and methods (Applied Social Research Methods, Vol. 5)*, Thousand Oaks, CA: Sage.

Further Reading

The viva and doctoral assessment

Ballard, B. (1996) 'Contexts of judgment: an analysis of some assumptions identified in examiners' reports on 62 successful PhD theses', paper to the Conference on Quality in Postgraduate Research, Adelaide.

Bourke, S., Hattie, J. and Anderson, L. (2004) 'Predicting examiner recommendations on PhD theses', *International Journal of Educational Research*, 27(4), 178–194.

Carter, S. (2011) 'How to examine a thesis', *MAI Review*, 1, 1–3.

Hartley, J. and Fox, C. (2002) 'The viva experience: examining the examiners', *Higher Education Review*, 35(1), 24–30.

Johnston, S. (1997) 'Examining the examiners: an analysis of examiners' reports on doctoral theses', *Studies in Higher Education*, 22, 333–347.

Murray, R. (2009) *How to Survive your Viva*, Maidenhead: Open University Press.

Nightingale, P. (1984) 'Examination of research theses', *Higher Education Research and Development*, 3, 137–150.

Park, C. (2003) 'Levelling the playing field: towards best practice in the doctoral viva', *Higher Education Review*, 36(1), 22–44.

Pearce, L. (2005) *How to Examine a Thesis*, Maidenhead: McGraw-Hill International.

Pitkethly, A. and Prosser, M. (1995) 'Examiners' comments on the international context of PhD theses', in C. McNaught and K. Beattie (eds) *Research into Higher Education: Dilemmas, directions and diversions*, Melbourne: Higher Education Research and Development Society of Australasia Victoria).

Ryder, N. (2013) *Fail your Viva: Twelve steps to failing your PhD viva (and 58 tips for passing)*, Nathan Ryder.

Tinkler, P. and Jackson, C. (2002) 'In the dark? Preparing for the PhD viva', *Quality Assurance in Education*, 10(2), 86–97.

Yates, P. and Crossouard, B. (2007) 'The viva voce as cultural practice: the production of academic subjects'. Paper presented at the annual conference of the Society for Research into Higher Education (SRHE), Warwick.

The PhD

Cryer, P. (2006) *The Research Student's Guide to Success*, Maidenhead: Open University Press.

Delamont, S., Atkinson, P. and Parry, O. (2000) *The Doctoral Experience: Success and failure in graduate school*, London: Falmer Press.

Evans, C. and Stevenson, K. (2011) 'The experience of international nursing students studying for a PhD in the U.K.: a qualitative study', *BMC Nursing*, 10(11), www.biomedcentral.com/1472-6955/10/11.

Golde, C.M. and Dore, T.M. (2001) 'At cross purposes: what the experiences of doctoral students reveal about doctoral education'. A report for The Pew Charitable Trusts, Philadelphia, www.phd-survey.org/report.htm (accessed 18 July 2012).

Leonard, D., Becker, R. et al. (2005) 'To prove myself at the highest level: the benefits of doctoral study', *Higher Education Research and Development*, 24(2), 135–149.

Park, C. (2007) *Redefining the Doctorate*, York: The Higher Education Academy.

Petre, M. and Rugg, G. (2010) *The Unwritten Rules of PhD Research*, 2nd edn, Maidenhead: Open University Press.

Phillips, E.M. (1992) 'The concept of quality in the PhD', in D.J. Cullen (ed.) *Quality in PhD Education*, Canberra: Centre for Educational Development and Methods, Australian National University.

Phillips, E.M. and Pugh, D.S. (2000) *How to Get a PhD: A handbook for students and their supervisors*, Buckingham: Open University Press.

Rugg, G. and Petre, M. (2004) *The Unwritten Rules of PhD Research*, Maidenhead: Open University Press.

Verger, J. (1999) 'Doctor, doctoratus', *Lexikon des Mittelalters*, 3, Stuttgart: J.B. Metzler

Wellington, J., Bathmaker, A., Hunt, C., McCulloch, G. and Sikes, P. (2005) *Succeeding with your Doctorate*, London: Sage.

Wisker, G., Robinson, G., Trafford, V. and Warnes, M. (2002) 'Getting there in the end: contributions to the achievement of the PhD', in M. Kiley and G. Mullins (eds) *Quality in Postgraduate Research: Integrating perspectives*, Canberra: CELTS, University of Canberra.

Wright, T. and Cochrane, R. (2000) 'Factors influencing successful submission of PhD theses', *Studies in Higher Education*, 25(2), 181–195.

Practice-based and professional doctorates

Barnes, T. (2011) 'The engineering doctorate' in A. Fell, K. Flint and I. Haines, *Professional Doctorates in the UK*, UK Council for Graduate Education.

Bourner, T., Bowden, R. et al. (2001) 'Professional doctorates in England', *Studies in Higher Education*, 26(1), 65–83.

Burgess, H. and Wellington, J. (2010) 'Exploring the impact of the professional doctorate on students' professional practice and personal development: early indications', *Work-based Learning e-Journal*, 1(1), 161–176.

Costley, C. and Lester, S. (2012) 'Work-based doctorates: professional extension at the highest levels', *Studies in Higher Education*, 37(3), 257–269.

Fell, A., Flint, K. and Haines, I. (2011) *Professional Doctorates in the UK*. UK Council for Graduate Education.

Fulton, J., Kuit, J., Sanders, G. and Smith, P. (2012) 'The role of the professional doctorate in developing professional practice', *Journal of Nursing Management*, 20(1), 130–139.

Maxwell, T.W. and Shanahan, P.J. (1997) 'Towards a reconceptualisation of the doctorate: issues arising from comparative data relating to the EdD degree in Australia', *Studies in Higher Education*, 22(2), 133–149.

Maxwell, T.W. and Kupczyk-Romanczuk, G. (2009) 'The professional doctorate: defining the portfolio as a legitimate alternative to the dissertation', *Innovations in Education and Training International*, 46(2), 135–145.

Powell, S. and Long, E. (2005) *Professional Doctorate Awards in the UK*, UK Council for Graduate Education.

Ranney, K. (2012) 'Integrating theory and practice in a fine art doctorate', 3rd International Conference on Professional Doctorates, 2–3 April 2012, Florence, Italy. Middlesex University & UK Council for Graduate Education.

Sanders, G., Kuit, J., Smith, P., Fulton, J. and Curtis, H. (2011) 'Identity, reflection and developmental networks as processes in professional doctorate development', *Work Based Learning e-Journal*, 2(1).

Winter, R., Griffiths, M. and Green, K. (2000) 'The "academic" qualities of practice: what are the criteria for a practice-based PhD?', *Studies in Higher Education*, 25, 25–37.

Useful Web Resources

Quality Assurance Agency

www.qaa.ac.uk

The Quality Assurance Agency for Higher Education (QAA) aims to safeguard standards and improve the quality of UK higher education. QAA offers 'advice, guidance and support to help UK universities, colleges and other institutions provide the best possible student experience of higher education'. It publishes a range of reference documents which promote best practice and standards (including doctoral standards). For example; the UK Quality Code for Higher Education (the Quality Code) sets out the expectations that all providers of UK higher education are required to meet.

Vitae

www.vitae.ac.uk

Vitae's mission is to lead world-class career and professional development of researchers. It works in partnership with higher education institutions, research organisations, funders and national organisations to 'meet society's need for high-level skills and innovation and produce world-class researchers'. Vitae is supported by Research Councils UK (RCUK), UK HE funding bodies and managed by CRAC (The Career Development Organisation), and delivered in partnership with regional hub host universities. The website has a section for postgraduate researchers, which includes the very useful Vitae Researcher Development Framework. There are also tips on preparing for your viva, including a viva checklist.

PhD comics

phdcomics.com/comics.php

Piled Higher and Deeper (also known as PhD Comics) is a great fun newspaper and web comic strip written and drawn by Jorge Cham that follows the lives of several graduate students. First published in 1997 when Cham was a graduate student at Stanford University, the strip deals with issues of life in graduate school, including the difficulties of scientific research, the perils of procrastination, the complex student–supervisor relationship and the endless search for free food.

National Postgraduate Committee (NPC)

www.npc.org.uk

The NPC is a charity to advance, in the public interest, postgraduate education in the UK. It is made up of postgraduate student representatives from educational institutions with postgraduate students. The NPC aims to promote the interests of postgraduates studying in the UK, holds an annual conference and publishes various guidelines and codes of practice.

The Postgraduate Forum

www.postgraduateforum.com

The UK Postgraduate Forum is an online forum which has been set up to 'help current, future and previous postgraduate students to exchange ideas, get advice and generally help each other out.' You will find lots of discussions about PhD studies.

The Thesis Whisperer

thesiswhisperer.com

The Thesis Whisperer is a blog newspaper dedicated to the topic of doing a thesis and is edited by Dr Inger Mewburn, Director of Research Training at the Australian National University. It includes some excellent pages and some very good tips and advice for preparing for your viva.

UK Council for Graduate Education (UKCGE)

www.ukcge.ac.uk/main/home

UKCGE is an independent representative body for Postgraduate Education in the UK. Its mission is to be 'the authoritative voice for postgraduate education in the UK, providing high quality leadership and support to its members to promote a strong and sustainable postgraduate education sector.' The UKCGE produces best practice documents and runs regular events and conferences.

The Society for Research into Higher Education (SRHE)

www.srhe.ac.uk

SRHE is a UK-based international learned society which is 'concerned to advance understanding of higher education, especially through the insights, perspectives and knowledge offered by systematic research and scholarship. The Society aims to be the leading international society in the field, as to both the support and the dissemination of research.' SRHE runs a series of conferences which have included several papers on the PhD and doctoral experiences.

The Speed PhD

www.mhs.manchester.ac.uk/postgraduate/skillstrainingsupport/
videosgstp/videoprofiles

'The Speed PhD' is a two-day training course for first-year research students, which was originally designed and implemented at Manchester University, but is now used at various institutions across the UK. It uses group activities to simulate the PhD process, from starting a doctorate through to the viva, in a two-day course.

Higher Education Academy

www.heacademy.ac.uk

The Higher Education Academy champions excellent learning and teaching in higher education. It is an independent organisation, funded by the four UK HE funding bodies and by subscriptions and grants. It has published a number of best practice papers relating to the doctorate. If you search on the website using the word 'doctorate' you will find several items which may interest you.

Marian van Bakel's blog

marianvanbakel.wordpress.com/2013/02/27/
defending-your-phd-thesis-the-dutch-way/comment-page-1

This blog (reproduced, with Marian's permission, within this book) presents an account of Marian's PhD defence.

Jenna Condie's blog

socphd.wordpress.com/2013/06/07/
dont-mock-the-mock-the-importance-of-a-having-a-practice-viva

This blog (reproduced, with Jenna's permission, within this book) presents an account of Jenna's mock viva.

Professor Simon Leather's blog: Are PhD examiners really ogres?

simonleather.wordpress.com/2013/05/07/
are-phd-examiners-really-ogres

This blog (reproduced, with Simon's permission, within this book) presents his thoughts and experiences on PhD assessment. Professor Leather is a very experienced PhD examiner.

Index